BAKUNIN

BAKUNIN

The Philosophy of Freedom

Brian Morris

BLACK ROSE BOOKS

Montréal/New York
London

BLACK ROSE BOOKS No. W192
Hardcover ISBN 1-895431-67-0
Paperback ISBN 1-895431-66-2

Library of Congress No. 93-70390

Canadian Cataloguing in Publication Data

Morris, Brian, 1936–
Bakunin : the philosophy of freedom

ISBN 1-895431-67-0 (bound) –
ISBN 1-895431-66-2 (pbk.)

1. Bakunin, Mikhail Aleksandrovich, 1814–1876. 2. Anarchism. I. Title.

HX914.7.B34M67   1993   320.5'7'092   C93-090101-0

Cover Design: Nat Klym

Mailing Address

BLACK ROSE BOOKS
C.P. 1258
Succ. Place du Parc
Montréal, Québec
H2W 2R3 Canada

BLACK ROSE BOOKS
340 Nagel Drive
Cheektowaga, New York
14225 USA

Printed in Canada

A publication of the Institute of Policy Alternatives of Montréal
(IPAM)

Contents

To Ketta, Dodo and Erica.

The present is where we get lost — if we forget our past and have no vision of the future.

Ayi Kwei Armah. *The Healers* (1978).

Preface

BAKUNIN, like "reason" and "atheism," is currently out of fashion. Nowadays, he tends to be treated as some historical curiosity. Marxists dismiss him as a misguided romantic with a bent for destruction and secret societies, and pour scorn on his alleged "elitist despotism." Liberal scholars on the other hand, continue to find Bakunin fascinating—but only as a subject for studies in utopian or Freudian psychology. Surprisingly, even anarchists appear to have lost interest in Bakunin. There seems to be a foreboding feeling that any interest in such historical figures as Bakunin is a distraction, and that we should concern ourselves with more contemporary issues—like the deconstructionism of Derrida, sociobiology and postmodernism.

Bakunin surely deserves better treatment. For myself, I tend to agree with the radical scholar, Cedric Robinson, namely, that our "shared past" is precious to us not only for itself but because it is the basis of consciousness, of knowing, of being, and has salience in our struggles for a better world. Bakunin is a crucial part of this "shared past."

His legacy is an important one, and his ideas, as Paul Avrich and many others have suggested, have a contemporary relevance—particularly his critiques of Marxism and scientism. They certainly have more relevance than sociobiology and the musings of many postmodernists.

More than a decade has passed since Sam Dolgoff and Arthur Lehning produced their important anthologies of Bakunin's writings. It seems to be the right time to reaffirm Bakunin's stature and significance. This is the aim of the present study. It is not meant to be a scholarly work—simply a readable guide to the life and work of Michael Bakunin—a major political figure and the real inspiration of libertarian socialism and the anarchist movement.

Brian Morris
Lewes, Sussex
March, 1993

Part One: A Biographical Sketch

Chapter 1

Bakunin: His Personality

MICHAEL BAKUNIN was an extraordinary man, and his life and personality still continue to fascinate scholars even though there is still no biography that does him full justice. E. H. Carr's classic study, though providing a good outline of Bakunin's life, demonstrates little real sympathy for his subject, and fails to examine what is historically important about Bakunin: not his flamboyant personality but rather the theory of libertarian socialism that he developed during the last years of his life. Bakunin was not an intellectual—if anything, he was anti-intellectual—and so never produced a systematic account of his ideas in the manner of Marx or Herbert Spencer. But his thoughts are by no means incoherent, and he deserves to be recognized as an important and influential political theorist. For he was not only in his own lifetime the embodiment of the Russian radical ethos—having an important influence on Russian populism—but he was one of the first to propound a coherent theory of communist anarchism.

Physically, Bakunin was a giant, full of energy, who exercised a volcanic force, and often fascinated all those with whom he came into contact. "Everything about him was colossal," the composer Richard Wagner recalled, for he was "full of a primitive exuberance and strength."[1] He lived a totally disordered life, living mostly off his friends from whom he continually borrowed money, none of which was ever repaid. He was "monumentally eccentric" and had enormous appetites; he smoked incessantly, drank endless cups of tea, and quaffed brandy like wine. He had no sense of time or order, and virtually no sense of property and material security or comfort. He invariably slept with his clothes on. His lifestyle never changed. As his life-long friend Alexander Herzen wrote in his *Memoirs*:

> His activity, his laziness, his appetite, his titanic stature and the everlasting perspiration he was in, everything about him, in fact, was on a superhuman scale. He remained as of old a blue-eyed giant with a leonine head and a tousled mane. At fifty he was exactly the same vagrant student, the same harmless bohemian . . . with no thought of the mor-

row, careless of money, flinging it away when he had it,
borrowing it indiscriminantly right and left, when he had
not, as simply as children take from their parents, careless
of repayment; as simply as he himself would give his last
shilling to anyone, only keeping what he needed for
cigarettes and tea. This manner of life did not worry him;
he was born to be the great vagrant, the great outcast.

And Herzen continues:

There was something childlike, simple and free from
malice about him, and this gave him extraordinary charm
and attracted both the weak and the strong, repelling none
but the stiff petty-bourgeois. His striking personality, the
eccentric and powerful appearance he made everywhere
. . . makes him one of those original figures which neither
the contemporary world nor history can pass by.[2]

As a result of his aristocratic background, Bakunin was cos-
mopolitan in outlook and despite his privileged upbringing, totally un-
conscious of class barriers, mixing freely with all kinds of people, and
with children. This was facilitated by the fact that Bakunin had a good
command of European languages, speaking English, Italian, German,
French and Spanish, as well as Russian.[3]

Bakunin was by all accounts an evidently lovable man, and inspired deep affection among his friends. G. D. H. Cole writes of him:

He was eminently genial, almost incapable of taking of-
fence, and utterly irresponsible. He was also a most loyal
friend and very generous in praise of his opponents, if he
regarded them as belonging fundamentally to the "side"
of the revolution—which was his passion. He spoke most
generously of Marx's services to the cause, even when
they were in sharp conflict and when Marx was reviling
him and accusing him of all manner of crimes, besides
those of which he was guilty. He praised Nechaev's good
qualities, even when Nechaev had stolen his private
papers and thrown him over after making all the use he
could of the old man's patronage. He was indeed as incapable of meanness and malice as of ordinary bourgeois
honesty in matters of money.[4]

But Bakunin was also full of contradictions and always remained something of an enigma to his contemporaries. He was highly intelligent and yet, at the same time, naive and gullible; he breathed an air of revolt and freedom and yet had an insatiable urge to be dominant in personal relationships. Bakunin was aware of this. "Despite my love of freedom," he wrote to his brother Paul, "I had a great tendency to despotism." Frankness, Lampert writes, "was Bakunin's characteristic trait"[5] As Bakunin was also prone to making confessions, he is an ideal subject for those biographers who wish to imply that his rebellious spirit was a function of his disorderly personality, or who wish to denigrate him. A typical example of the latter is Aileen Kelly's (1982) study of "utopian psychology." She is interested neither in Bakunin as a person, nor in his anarchism (which she dismissed in cavalier fashion as of "little merit"). Her book is one long diatribe against Bakunin, who she portrays as fanatical, gullible, vindictive, megalomaniac, an idealist and romantic dilettante who lived in a fantasy world and was completely out of touch with reality. Bakunin, was, she implies, the prototype of the alienated intellectual. She is obsessive in her dislike of Bakunin, and is quite unable to find anything positive to say about Bakunin's personality or his ideas. Kelly's study is thus scholastic and not a work of scholarship. In fact, Kelly herself exemplifies the kind of personality she attempts to foist upon Bakunin: the detached intellectual with a "personal obsession" who imposes abstract categories and interpretations on the empirical reality. Bakunin had a much more vivid sense of the world and its contradictions than Kelly has of Bakunin and his times. The studies of Lampert (1957) and Masters (1974) seem to me to be much closer to the truth about Bakunin, though not uncritical.

However, the contradictions in Bakunin's life and character need to be stressed. Max Nomad, whose tendency as a historian is to see all nineteenth-century revolutionaries as power-hungry personalities— which is misleading to say the least—sums up these contradictions rather succinctly:

> A Russian nobleman of royal ancestry, he was the most eloquent champion of the peasants in revolt against their feudal and semi-feudal masters. Born to wealth, he preferred the life of a homeless wanderer living on the bounty of his friends and followers. A despot and authoritarian by nature, he was the teacher of a gospel that rejected all authority, all compulsion. An internationalist in the scope of his activities, he was at heart a Slavic

chauvinist who hated and loathed the Germans and Jews. A self-confessed disciple of Karl Marx, he was his most bitter enemy. More famous and influential than his teacher during his lifetime, he was to shrink to the stature of a mere icon of a dying sect. The real grandfather and the precursor of Bolshevism, he has been denied by his grandchildren, who even begrudge him a monument.[6]

As we shall see, Bakunin was more than a "mere icon" to a dying sect. And to stress the contradictions and to see him as a precursor of Bolshevism is to fail to understand the underlying purpose of his life and the development of his political thought.

Bakunin, undoubtedly, was a visionary and a prophet, and as Carr describes him, "one of the completest embodiments in history of the spirit of liberty."[7] He had great vision and extraordinary magnetism and a "demonic capacity for communicating ideas." His friend Belinsky acknowledges in Bakunin "a power and depth of spirit, a remarkable mobility of mind, extraordinary gifts, an infinite capacity for understanding," while at the same time stressing his limitations—an inability to love, a desire to subjugate others, naivety, a tremendous pride and egoism. "A bulky piece of Neanderthal humanity" is how Lampert describes Bakunin[8]—elemental, rebellious, disordered, spontaneous, enthusiastic. He was, in the words of a contemporary, like a "great ship, without rudder, drifting before the wind and not knowing why or whither." But his drifting was motivated by a vision of liberty, and his spiritual restlessness was eventually to find fulfilment in the last years of his life when he sketched out a new political philosophy—a revolutionary socialism.

NOTES

1. Carr, E. H. 1937. *Michael Bakunin*. New York: Knopf, p. 196.
2. Lampert, E. 1957. *Studies in Rebellion*. London: Routledge & Kegan Paul, pp.112-113
3. Carr, op. cit. p. 465.
4. Cole, G.D.H., 1954. *History of Socialist Thought, Vol. II, Marxism and Anarchism 1850-1890*. London: Macmillan, p. 219.
5. Lampert, op. cit., p.113.
6. Nomad, M. 1933. *Apostles of Revolution*. New York: Collier, p. 151.
7. Carr, op. cit., p. 457.
8. Lampert, op. cit., p. 120.

Chapter 2

Early Years: 1814-1849

MIKHAIL ALEKSANDROVICH BAKUNIN was born on May 18, 1814 in Premukhino, a small village in the province of Tver, situated about one hundred and fifty miles northwest of Moscow. His father was a wealthy landowner who had spent his early years as a career diplomat in Italy, after graduating as a Doctor of Philosophy from the University of Padua. He had liberal tendencies and is described as "humane, cultured, intelligent, devoted to his home and family, but devoid of imagination and possessed of that touch of fanaticism proper to the frightened liberal."[1] Upon his return to Russia, Alexander Bakunin settled down to manage the family estates, and at the age of forty married a young woman of eighteen, Varvara Muraviev, who belonged to one of the most distinguished families in Russia. The family had liberal tendencies and some of its members became implicated in the Decembrist uprising of 1825. Between the years 1811 and 1824, Varvara became the mother of eleven children. Michael was the third child and the eldest boy, and throughout his childhood and youth had a close and intimate relationship with his four sisters who formed an elder group of siblings. Bakunin's early years were spent amid idyllic surroundings. As Max Nettlau writes:

> The absence of any economic problems, the comfortable country life among the bounties of nature, though it was based on the serfdom of many, formed a close bond between these sisters and brothers, created a microcosm of freedom and solidarity with intimate and intensive striving toward the inner perfection of each one of them and the full expression of his inborn talents.[2]

Nettlau suggests that it was here at the estate that the seeds of Bakunin's lifelong striving for freedom and solidarity were planted. Premukhino, Carr notes, was the very home and essence of the romantic spirit, where idyllic peace reigned, undisturbed by the harsh realities of the "external" world. It provided the "spiritual birthright" that Bakunin never forswore.

At the age of fifteen, Bakunin entered the Artillery Cadet School in St. Petersburg, and three years later was commissioned as a junior officer. But he didn't take to army life and after a violent quarrel with a general, he was posted to the provinces of Minsk and Grodno, in Poland. He arrived there shortly after the Polish insurrection of 1832 had been crushed , and was greatly disturbed by these events. He fell sick, and eventually obtained a discharge from the army at the end of 1835. His father tried to get Bakunin a position in the civil service in Tver, but his son refused, and early in 1836 Bakunin went to Moscow to establish an independent life. He intended to study philosophy and to earn a living by teaching mathematics. In those days, the University of Moscow, in contrast to St. Petersburg which had become, after the Decembrist uprising, a "citadel of reaction," was a veritable haven of intellectual activity.[3] German idealist philosophy, associated with Fichte, Schelling and Hegel was then all the rage in Russia, and, as in Germany, tended to take prominence over social and political discussions.

Bakunin lived in Moscow for the next six years, spending some of the summer vacations on the family estate at Premukhino. Interested in the possibility of becoming a professor, he studied philosophy as well as reading the French Encyclopaedists. He became fascinated with the philosophical ideas of Fichte whose book *Guide to the Blessed Life* became his constant companion. His letter to his sisters of that period express the important influence of Fichte's romantic philosophy on Bakunin, and he also translated Fichte's *On the Vocation of the Scholar* into Russian with the translation appearing in one of the leading intellectual journals. During that period in Moscow two discussion "circles" met secretly to discuss philosophical issues. One, associated with Alexander Herzen and Nicholas Ogarev, tended to be more concerned with politics and found its spiritual home in the French utopian socialists. The other, which was known as the "circle of Stankevich," eschewed politics and devoted itself to discussion of German metaphysical philosophy and German poetry. Bakunin joined Nicholas Stankevich's circle and he and Stankevich soon became firm friends. Vissarion Belinsky also joined the circle, and he too became a close friend and confidant of Bakunin. Belinsky was destined to become one of the great literary critics of his generation. Stankevich was considered one of the few men in Russia who really understood German idealist philosophy; he has been described as one of the intellectual luminaries of his generation.[4] Both men were friends and early disciples of Bakunin, and became intimately involved with the Bakunin family.

Both died of tuberculosis at an early age: Stankevich in 1840 at age twenty-seven and Belinsky in 1848 at age thirty-seven. Bakunin shared Belinsky's and Stankevich's enthusiasm for Fichte, as this philosopher expressed the pure romantic spirit, carrying the idealism of Kant to an extreme subjectivism, the self being virtually equated with the absolute ego. In his letters to his sisters, Bakunin expounded Fichte's philosophy. To one of his sisters he wrote that "one must wholly annihilate one's personal ego, annihilate everything that forms its life, its hopes and its personal beliefs. One must live and breath only for the absolute through the absolute."[5] Fichte, Bakunin was to write, is "the true hero of our time. I have always loved him deeply, and have envied his extraordinary power."[6] Kelly fails to understand that Bakunin grew out of his youthful mysticism. In fact, his enthusiasm for Fichte did not last very long, for early in 1837 Bakunin began his studies of Hegel.

Hegel is a difficult scholar to understand, but Bakunin applied himself to Hegel's writings with diligence. After consulting a textbook on Hegel's system of logic, he tackled the works of Hegel himself, beginning with the *Phenomenology of Spirit*. He soon abandoned this in favour of the Encyclopaedia, and thus first encountered the famous phrase that has long baffled the followers of Hegel: "That which is rational is real, and that which is real is rational." Equating the real with existence, some had come to see this maxim as a justification for the Prussian State. Bakunin came to interpret Hegel rather differently. But like Marx, he accepted Hegel's philosophy with enthusiasm, particularly as it contrasted with Fichte's romanticism by taking into account external reality. Hegel is giving me an entirely new life, he wrote to his sister, "I am completely absorbed by him." From Hegel, as Venturi put it, Bakunin was able to find a reconciliation with reality, which was neither religious abandon nor an absorption in empirical problems.[7] Bakunin possessed a quick and receptive brain, and contrary to what Carr implies, his knowledge of Hegelian philosophy was thorough and serious.[8] What was of particular importance for Bakunin in Hegel's philosophy was his dialectical method, and his notion of a "true harmony," the overcoming of the opposition between the individual subject and society (spirit). But this "wholeness"—holism—implied a dialectical unity that Bakunin was later to articulate in his theory of anarchism. It did not suggest—as Kelly misleadingly interprets both Hegel and Bakunin—the "merging of consciousness and will with a transcendent whole."[9] This is pure mysticism which both Hegel and Bakunin renounced. She writes in a significant paragraph:

> This millenarian vision of liberty is an extraordinary
> abstract one; the ideal of wholeness as the resolution of
> all duality and conflict, the identity of the individual and
> the social, is a totally intransigent negation of all existing
> reality, a form of mystical anarchism.[10]

She is correct in suggesting that Bakunin's early Hegelianism left a permanent mark on his outlook, but the above statement indicates an abysmal ignorance of what both Hegel and Bakunin stood for, as both came to repudiate such mystical idealism, and the "identity" theory of Schelling and Fichte. Hegel had a profound influence on Russian culture during the 1830s: Bakunin felt this influence deeply, and like Marx, imbibed its central tenets. He clearly understood Hegel better than his biographer!

The year 1838 was an eventful one for Bakunin. His sister Lyubov died of tuberculosis, Stankevich had gone abroad with his other sister Varvara, and a quarrel with his friend Belinsky—one of the most intelligent and warmhearted of all the friends of Bakunin's early manhood—had led to the end of their friendship. Belinsky, like Stankevich, was to stress in his letters the extreme ambiguities in Bakunin's personality—a man so lovable, and with so much strength, energy and purpose—and yet a man who lacked a certain tenderness in his personal relationships. Bakunin "loves ideas, not men. He wants to dominate with his personality, not to love," wrote Belinsky.[11] During the winter of 1839-40 in Moscow, the last Bakunin was to spend in Russia, Bakunin came into contact with two men who were later to play a substantial role in his life. These were Alexander Herzen and Nicholas Ogarev. Both came, like Bakunin, from rich landowning families. Both were radical intellectuals who had only recently returned to Moscow after spending several years in exile. Bakunin found both men stimulating company but at that period they exerted little influence on him. For he was still immersed in philosophical studies and had the feeling that he would "gradually decay mentally" if he stayed in Russia. His personal life was also at a low ebb. So he decided to go to Berlin, to study Hegelian philosophy at its source. His motivations for leaving Russia combined both a yearning for more knowledge and a need to escape from personal disappointments. He expresses this in a letter to his friend, the ailing Stankevich (February 1840):

> My whole life, my whole virtue have consisted of a sort of
> abstract spiritual force, and that force has been ship-

wrecked on the sordid trivial ties of everyday family life, of
empty family quarrels, and of quarrels between friends,
and perhaps also on my own incapacity. There still sur-
vives within me the old strong need, predominating over
everything else, for living knowledge—a thirst which is
still unsatisfied despite all my poor, laborious efforts.[12]

Bakunin managed to convince his father that he should support
Bakunin's studies in Germany for three years, so that he could obtain a
doctorate, which would then enable him to return to the University of
Moscow as a professor. His father agreed to give him an allowance of
1,500 rubles a year. And so, in June 1840, at the age of twenty-six,
Bakunin left Russia for Germany. At the end of the month he learned
that Stankevich had died in Italy which came as a terrible blow to
Bakunin, for Stankevich had been a rather saintly person as well as a
brilliant scholar—and he had been a true friend to Bakunin. He had
died in the arms of Bakunin's sister, Varvara, who then moved to Berlin
to set up house with Bakunin, and with his new-found friend Ivan Tur-
genev. Bakunin had reached a transition point in his life. As Venturi
writes:

When he finally went abroad in 1840, Bakunin had
broken with everyone. He felt isolated. His political conceptions remained those of a conservative by philosophical choice; his ideas were those of a convinced Hegelian.
Yet he felt profoundly dissatisfied. He was now in agreement with no one.[13]

He immersed himself in philosophical studies, attending the lectures
on Hegel at the University of Berlin, given by one of Hegel's orthodox
disciples. Bakunin also met Schelling and attended his lectures, but he
was unimpressed by these. They were "uninteresting but rather insig-
nificant," he noted. The same year that Bakunin arrived in Berlin—
1840—Wilhelm IV became the King of Prussia. He proved to be a highly
reactionary monarch, and began the persecution of many radicals. The
following year, Feuerbach published his famous study, *The Essence of
Christianity.* It offered a purely materialist interpretation of religion, and
made a tremendous impact upon his contemporaries. "One must have
experienced the liberating effect of this book to get an idea of it," wrote
Friedrich Engels. "Enthusiasm was general; we all became at once Feuer-
bachians. How enthusiastically Marx greeted this new conception and

how much he was influenced by it."[14] Feuerbach's book became the
rallying-point for a group of radicals who became known as the "Left
Hegelians"; they argued that Hegel's philosophy was not an ideology
of reaction, but was essentially a revolutionary doctrine. Bakunin
became associated with the Left Hegelians, coming under the influence
of Arnold Ruge, who was a republican and an atheist.

By the spring of 1842, Bakunin had given up the idea of becoming a
university professor and had moved to Dresden to join Ruge. In October he published an article in Ruge's journal, "Deutsche Jahrbucher"
(German Yearbook). It was written under the pseudonym of Jules
Elysard, and entitled "Reaction in Germany: From the Notebooks of a
Frenchman." This brilliant essay, in spite of its Hegelian emphasis, is
generally acknowledged to be one of Bakunin's best literary works. It is
a polemical essay; in it Bakunin argues against the defenders of reaction, which finds its theoretical expression in the positive philosophy of
Comte. The realization of liberty, Bakunin writes, "today stands at the
head of the agenda of history." No one openly admits to being the
enemy of freedom, he notes, yet there are many people who, in their in-
nermost hearts, do not believe in liberty. These are the reactionaries.
They support the status quo, either as conformists or compromisers.
But the important thing about Hegel's philosophy, Bakunin argues, is
his stress on the negative, which has not only a logical but a historical
significance. This negation expressed itself in the spirit of revolution.
Everywhere, but especially in England and France, there are social forces emerging which are wholly alien to the present political world.

> The people, the poor class, which without doubt con-
> stitute the greatest part of humanity; the class whose
> rights have already been recognized in theory but which
> is nevertheless still despised for its birth, for its ties with
> poverty and ignorance as well as indeed with actual
> slavery—this class is everywhere assuming a threatening
> attitude. All people and all men are filled with a kind of
> premonition . . . even in Russia dark clouds are gathering
> and heralding a storm. Oh, the air is sultry and pregnant
> with lightning.

And the essay concludes with the famous words:

> Let us therefore trust the eternal spirit which destroys
> and annihilates only because it is the unfathomable and

eternal source of all life. The passion for destruction is a creative passion too![15]

This essay marks a shift in Bakunin's thinking, away from philosophy and towards revolutionary politics. Carr suggests that it represents Bakunin's "farewell to Hegel,"[16] although this is perhaps a little too sweeping. It made, however, a profound impression on Herzen and Belinsky and created something of a sensation in European revolutionary circles.[17]

While in Dresden, Bakunin became friends with a young radical German poet, Georg Herwegh, as well as with the musician, Adolf Reichel. And it was in Dresden that he first became acquainted with French socialism. He had read Lamennais's *Politique du peuple* as well as Van Stein's *Socialism and Communism in Contemporary France*, which outlined the theories of Saint-Simon, Fourier and Proudhon. But it was his meeting with Wilhelm Weitling in May 1843, during a short sojourn in Zurich, that provided Bakunin with an important "catalyst" in the formation of his ideas. Weitling was an extraordinary figure. He came from a modest background, the illegitimate son of a young German woman and a French officer. He was a tailor by trade but wanting to evade military service, he had wandered from country to country. He settled in Paris in 1835 and there studied French revolutionary socialism. Expelled from Paris four years later, he took refuge in Switzerland. Like Bakunin he was a wanderer. Bakunin had read his book *Guarantees of Harmony and Freedom* (1842) and was greatly impressed by it. He quoted to Ruse a striking passage from the book: "The perfect society had no government, but only an administration, no laws, but only obligations, no punishments, but only means of correction."[18]

It is suggested that here in embryonic form was the anarchist creed that Bakunin himself was later to advocate.[19] Relations between Bakunin and Weitling were warm and friendly, for both were activists and had "plenty of undisciplined fanaticism." But Bakunin even during that early period, was critical of the kind of communism that Weitling advocated. Thus, he wrote in an article published in June 1843:

> Once and for all we announce that we are not communists. We have little desire to live in a State, built according to Weitling's plan, one which is not the expression of a free society, but rather a herd of animals organized by compulsion and force, and concerned solely with material interests, ignoring the spiritual side of life.[20]

Weitling was soon arrested and expelled from Switzerland. As Bakunin's name was found on some of Weitling's papers, and as he was known to be associated with such radicals as Ruge and Herwegh, Bakunin was ordered by the Russian Legation in Berne to return immediately to Russia. This Bakunin refused to do. Instead, he travelled to Brussels, and after staying there three months, he went on to Paris, arriving there in March 1844.

Paris at that time was a Mecca for revolutionaries and was full of "malcontents of many nationalities and of every school." Bakunin soon became acquainted with the French socialists and political and literary personalities of all shades of opinion. He was to live in Paris for three and a half years—until November 1847—and became associated with a number of important figures: the writer George Sand, the socialists Louis Blanc and Pierre Leroux, Étienne Cabet—the veteran socialist who had written the famous *Voyage en Icarie* (1840)—as well as Ruge and his old friends Reichel and Herwegh. But the two people Bakunin met in Paris who were destined to play a significant role in his life, and were important formative influences on him were Karl Marx and Pierre-Joseph Proudhon. Much has been written on the relationships between these three men. All were later to significantly influence the development of European socialism.

Bakunin's relationship with Proudhon was amicable. Proudhon, like Weitling, was a self-educated man of humble origins. He came from a peasant background, having been born in Besancon in 1809. He trained as a printer and in 1840 published the famous pamphlet, "What is property?"—giving as the answer Brissot's famous dictum, "property is theft." The pamphlet made him famous, and when Bakunin reached Paris, Proudhon was at the height of his success. His critique of property was complemented by a strident atheism and a disapproval of constitutional government. But Proudhon was not a socialist, for he stresses the importance of small-scale property holding. Bakunin and Proudhon often met and had long discussions—discussions which lasted through the night. Bakunin is said to have initiated Proudhon into Hegelian philosophy, for Proudhon spoke no German, and Hegel's writings had not been translated into French. There is no doubt that Proudhon—with his attacks on God, private property and the State—influenced Bakunin. And Bakunin always acknowledged his debt to Proudhon and held him in high esteem. "Proudhon," he wrote many years later, was "a hundred times more of a revolutionary in his actions and his instinct that the doctrinaire bourgeois socialists."[21] Many writers have emphasized the instrumental effect that Proudhon exerted on Bakunin. Eugène Pyziur, for instance, writes:

> It must be stressed that it was due to the influence of Proudhon's ideas that Bakunin's instinctive rebellionism was transformed into a formulated, doctrinaire, anarchist creed. It was Proudhon who provided Bakunin with the theorems and concepts which were essential to him in his later creation of a species of anarchist doctrine, when this became necessary for Bakunin in his duel with Marx.[22]

But this influence was reciprocal and Daniel Guerin (1986) has stressed that within the intimacy of this relationship, Bakunin both learned and taught. Yet, although Bakunin admired Proudhon and valued his friendship and defended him against the "filthy things" which Marx wrote against him, he was not uncritical of Proudhon's anarchism. In a French manuscript of 1870, Bakunin evaluates Proudhon, comparing him with Marx:

> As I told him a few months before his death, Proudhon, in spite of all his efforts to shake off the tradition of classical idealism, remained all of his life an incorrigible idealist, immersed in the Bible, in Roman law and metaphysics. His great misfortune was that he had never studied the natural sciences, or appropriated their method. He had the instincts of a genius, a revolutionary thinker, arguing against idealistic phantoms, and yet never able to surmount them himself. Marx as a thinker is on the right path. He has established the principle that juridical evolution in history is not the cause but the effect of economic development, and this is a great and fruitful concept. Though he did not originate it . . . to Marx belongs the credit of solidly establishing it as the basis for an economic system. On the other hand, Proudhon when not obsessed with metaphysical doctrine, was a revolutionary by instinct. Quite possibly Marx could construct a still more rational system of liberty but he lacks the instinct of liberty—he remains from head to foot an authoritarian.[23]

There was little closeness between Marx and Bakunin. They knew each other well for both belonged to the group of emigrés who were associated with the German weekly newspaper *Vorwärts*. They also had much in common. Both men had been deeply affected by Hegelian philosophy and admired the work of the poet Herwegh. Both disliked Ruge for his scheming, and were critical of the reactionary politics in Germany: for writing two anti-Prussian articles in *Vorwärts* (January 1845) Marx was expelled from France at the request of the Prussian government. But temperamentally and politically, Bakunin and Marx were poles apart. Marx was hard, meticulous and calculating and put a dominant emphasis on reason. Bakunin was spontaneous, extravagant and emotional. Marx was a Jewish lawyer's son from Rhineland; Bakunin a Russian aristocrat, and between them, Carr records, "there was not merely a clash of temperaments, but a lack of any common background of tradition and ideas; and from the outset they neither understood nor liked each other."[24] The rivalry between the two men, and their differing conception of socialism, was to later split the socialist movement, and lead to the demise of the First International. At the height of their disagreement (1871), Bakunin recalled his early encounters with Marx in Paris which are indicative that Bakunin was not lacking in a generous spirit and certainly not consumed by jealousy, as Kelly implies. He wrote:

> As far as learning was concerned, Marx was, and still is, incomparably more advanced than I. I knew nothing at that time of political economy, I had not yet rid myself of my metaphysical observations, and my socialism was only instinctive. Although younger than I, he was already an atheist, a conscious materialist and an informed socialist. It was precisely at this time that he was elaborating the foundations of his system as it stands today. We saw each other often, I greatly respected him for his learning and for his passionate devotion—though it was always mingled with vanity—to the cause of the proletariat. I eagerly sought his conversation, which was always instinctive and witty when it was not inspired by petty hate, which Alas! was only too often the case. There was never any frank intimacy between us—our temperaments did not permit it. He called me a sentimental idealist and he was right; I called him vain, perfidious and cunning, and I also was right.[25]

In November 1847, Bakunin made his first public speech. It was at a banquet attended by 1,500 Polish refugees, on the occasion of the anniversary of the Polish insurrection of 1831. An impressive orator, the speech marked a turning point in Bakunin's career. The speech created a sensation, and within a month Bakunin had been ordered to leave French territory. Already at the end of 1844, Tsar Nicholas I had issued a decree depriving Bakunin of his noble rank, confiscating all his property, and, in his absence, sentencing him to a period of hard labour in Siberia. Bakunin thus became a permanent exile. He left Paris for Brussels where Marx had been living since his expulsion from France. Marx at that time was organizing the Communist league; Bakunin took little interest in these activities, although he did join Marx's democratic Federation. He took an instinctive dislike to the German socialists associated with Marx, many of whom were Jews. He wrote to his friend Herwegh about the group:

> The German workers, Bornstadt, Marx, Engels—especially Marx—poison the atmosphere. Vanity, malevolence, gossip, pretentiousness and boasting in theory and cowardice in practice. Dissertations about life, action, and feeling—and complete absence of life, action, and feeling . . . the epithet "bourgeois!" is shouted ad nauseum by people who are from head to foot more bourgeois than anyone in a provincial city. In such an atmosphere one cannot breathe freely. I stay away from them and will have nothing to do with this organization.[26]

With the outbreak of the revolution in 1848, Bakunin returned to Paris and found accommodation among the working class national guard. Here he lodged for a week, and was enchanted with everything he heard and saw. "I breathed through all my senses and through all my pores the intoxication of the revolutionary atmosphere" he was later to recall. Bakunin was in his element as a wave of revolution spread throughout Europe, shaking the political and social order to its foundations. The revolution in Paris was a largely spontaneous affair, but it triggered off a series of revolutions throughout Europe. On March 18 there was a revolt against Austrian rule in Milan; the day before a constitutional government had been established in Hungary; and throughout Germany revolutionary discontent was widespread. Having persuaded the government to give him a loan of 2,000 francs— for revolutionary work—Bakunin left Paris at the end of March hoping to kindle the revolution in eastern Europe. He had by then espoused

Pan-Slavism as his revolutionary credo—a cause which he hoped would engender revolution throughout Europe. He made his way to Posen but was intercepted by the Prussian police, who escorted him to Leipzig. He then went on to Breslau and stayed there a month (May 1848), but nothing was happening and, disappointed, Bakunin moved on. Breslau was full of revolutionary Poles, but they were disorganized, and suspicious of Bakunin as the Tsarist agents had spread the rumour that Bakunin was one of their own spies—a rumour that Marx later published in his journal, the *Neue Rheinische Zeitung* (July 1848). The rumour was without foundation, and Marx's motives in publishing the accusation has often been questioned. It always disturbed Bakunin. After attending the Slav congress in Prague in June, Bakunin at last found refuge in the little town of Koethen, in the Duchy of Anhalt, which was at that time an oasis of liberal freedom in Germany. Here Bakunin wrote and printed one of his most famous works: "An Appeal to the Slavs."

The pamphlet calls for the unity of all Slavs and oppressed peoples and the dissolution of four Empires—"the States of the despots"—the Prussian, Austrian, Turkish and Russian. In their place a regeneration of Europe is invoked and the establishment of a "universal federation of European republics." There should be no other frontiers, Bakunin writes, "but those which respond simultaneously to nature and to justice, in accordance with the spirit of democracy—frontiers which the people themselves in their sovereign will shall trace, founded upon their national sympathies. Such was the unanimous cry of the peoples."[27]

And calling upon the slogans of the French revolution—liberty, equality and fraternity—Bakunin goes on to suggest that two great questions were posed in the spring of 1848.

> The social question, on the one hand, and the question of the independence of all the nations, the emancipation of the peoples, on the other, signifying emancipation within and outside. Everybody had come to the realization that liberty was merely a lie where the great majority of the population is reduced to a miserable existence, where, deprived of education, of leisure, and of bread, it is fated to serve as an underprop for the powerful and the rich. The social revolution, therefore, appears as a natural, necessary corollary of the political revolution. It has likewise been felt that, so long as there may be a single

persecuted nation in Europe, the decisive and complete triumph of democracy will not be possible anywhere. The oppression of one is the oppression of all, and one cannot violate the liberty of one without violating the freedom of all of us.[28]

Both Marx and Engels were critical of this pamphlet. Marx wrote that apart from the Russians and Poles "no Slavic people has a future" and Engels suggested that the southern Slavs—the Czechs, Slovaks, Serbs and Croats—were nothing but the "residual fragments of peoples," who never had a history of their own and "will never be able to achieve any kind of independence." With the overthrow of absolutism, Marx and Engels argued in the pages of *Neue Rheinische Zeitung*, of which Marx was editor, that only the "greatest historic nations"—Germany, Poland, Italy, Hungary—fulfilled the criteria for viable national States. Engels felt that among all Pan-Slavists "nationality took precedence over the revolution."[29] This could not be said of Bakunin, who was critical that Marx was unable to admit the right of the Slavs to free themselves from German domination. But Carr stresses the important similarities between Marx and Bakunin in their attitude to the 1848 revolutions. He writes:

> The revolution of 1848 had been the work of the bourgeoisie. Inspired by the traditional bourgeois watchwords of liberty and equality, it rejected aristocracy but was prepared to retain monarchy tempered by a constitution which assured the political and economic predominance of the bourgeoisie. It did not demand, and did not desire, the complete overthrow of the existing framework of society. The institution of private property was the bulwark of bourgeois supremacy; and when this bulwark was threatened, the bourgeoisie rallied to its defence as brutally and vindictively as the aristocracy had formerly rallied to the defence of its privileges. The proletariat wished to continue the revolution until every privilege, including that of the bourgeoisie had been swept away; and this new extension of the conception of revolution fumed the bourgeoisie at one stroke into counter-revolutionaries and defenders of privilege. In the summer and autumn of 1848, consistent radicals like Marx and Bakunin weighed the bourgeoisie in the revolutionary scales and found it wanting.

And he continues:

> Marx and Bakunin followed the same path. Constitution-
> al democracy was as inimical as privileged aristocracy to
> the cause of the revolution. Nothing but the overthrow
> of the whole social order would suffice.[30]

Bakunin had thus ended "Appeal to the Slavs" with the phrase:

> The social question thus appears to be first and foremost
> the question of the complete overthrow of society.[31]

In March 1849, Bakunin moved to Dresden in Saxony. There he met the composer Richard Wagner who was at that time conductor of the State Opera. He spent many hours at the house of Wagner and his wife Minna, and appears to have had a genuine interest in music. Bakunin particularly liked Beethoven, who is considered the musical interpreter of Hegel's philosophy. He also liked Wagner's own music. In May a popular rebellion broke out in Dresden, provoked by the King of Saxony who refused to accept the constitution for a democratic Germany approved by the Frankfurt parliament. The King fled, a provisional government was proclaimed and for five days the rebels controlled the city. The motives for the insurrection were of little interest to Bakunin—he had little sympathy for the bourgeois aims of the rebels. But he despised the Kings of Saxony and Prussia and prompted by Wagner, he soon joined the rebellion. He became totally involved in the struggle, showing considerable courage. After fierce fighting, the rebellion was put down by well- armed Prussian troops. The captured insurgents were shot on the spot or thrown into the Elbe. Bakunin escaped to Chemnitz. During the night of May 9, he was arrested by a group of armed bourgeoisie and handed over to the Saxon authorities. What Nettlau has described as a "long pilgrimage of agony" for Bakunin now began.

NOTES

1. Carr, E. H. 1937. *Michael Bakunin*, New York: Knopf, p. 7.
2. Maximoff, G. P. 1953. ed., *The Political Philosophy of Bakunin: Scientific Anarchism*. Glencoe: Free Press, p. 30.
3. Carr, op. cit., p. 30.

4. Kelly, A. 1982. *Mikhail Bakunin: A Study in the Psychology and Politics of Utopianism*, Oxford: Carendon Press, p. 29.
5. Kelly, op. cit., p. 38.
6. Venturi, F. 1960. *Roots of Revolution; A History of Populist & Socialist Movements in 19th Century Russia*, Trans. F. Haskell, University of Chicago Press, p. 39.
7. Venturi, op. cit., p. 40.
8. Pyziur, E. 1955. *The Doctrine of Anarchism of Michael Bakunin*, Milwaukee: Regnery, p. 24.
9. Kelly, op. cit., p. 20.
10. Kelly, op. cit., p. 21.
11. Carr, op. cit., p. 75.
12. Carr, op. cit., p. 85.
13. Venturi, op. cit., p. 43.
14. Marx, K. and Engels, F. 1968. *Selected Works*, London: Lawrence & Wishort, p. 592.
15. Dolgoff, S., ed., trans., introd., 1973. *Bakunin on Anarchy*, New York: Knopf, p. 57.
16. Carr, op. cit., p. 116.
17. Lampert, E. 1957. *Studies in Religion*, London: Routledge & Kegan Paul, p. 110.
18. Carr, op. cit., p. 127.
19. Carr, op. cit., p. 127.
20. Masters, A. 1974. *Bakunin: The Father of Anarchism*, London: Sidgwick and Jackson, p. 69.
21. Carr, op. cit., p. 137.
22. Pyziur, op. cit., p. 32.
23. Dolgoff, op. cit., p. 26.
24. Carr, op. cit., p. 136.
25. Dolgoff, op. cit., p. 25.
26. Dolgoff, op. cit., p. 27.
27. Dolgoff, op. cit., p. 66.
28. Dolgoff, op. cit., p. 68.
29. Munck, R. 1986. *The Difficult Dialogue: Marxism and Nationalism*. London: Zed Books, pp. 12-22.
30. Carr, op. cit. pp. 179-180.
31. Dolgoff, op. cit. p. 68.

Chapter 3

Prison and Exile: 1848-1861

B AKUNIN spent a year in Saxon prisons, first in Dresden then in the fortress of Koenigstein, where he was completely cut off from news of the outside world. He was tried, along with two of his associates, found guilty of treason, and sentenced to death. This was later commuted to life imprisonment. That his spirit was unbroken is evident from his letters to his friends Adolfe and Mathilde Reichel. In June 1850, he was wakened suddenly one night and driven to the Saxon boarder to be extradited to Austria. Bakunin did not know this and thought he was being taken to his place of execution. He was taken first to Prague, then to the hill fortress of Olmutz in Moravia, where he was fettered and chained to the wall of his cell. His physical condition began to deteriorate. Again he was tried by the judicial authorities, and found guilty of high treason—condemned in fact by his own writings as "Appeal to the Slavs" had advocated the complete destruction of the Austrian empire. He was sentenced to death by hanging as well as or-dered to pay the costs of the inquiry! But this was commuted to life im-prisonment, and he was again extradited—this time to Russia, something which Bakunin feared. He was taken by Cossacks to St. Petersburg and imprisoned in the fortress of Peter and Paul. As he had been tried and convicted of treason many years before Bakunin was taken across Russia as an already condemned prisoner.

He had already spent two years in various jails when in July 1851 Count Orlov, principal adviser to Nicholas I, appeared in Bakunin's cell. He brought a message from the Tsar assuring him that as the death penalty did not exist in Russia he had no reason to fear for his life, and invited Bakunin to write a full confession to the Tsar, as if he were a spiritual father. Thus, Bakunin came to write the famous and extraordi-nary document "Confession to the Tsar" (1851). The confession has al-ways proved useful to the detractors of Bakunin, for he openly pleads as a "repentant sinner" for the Tsar's forgiveness. But the contents of the document are highly ambiguous and if one takes into account the circumstances in which it was written it is difficult to condemn Bakunin. It is easy to see the confession as a piece of hypocrisy, designed to placate the Tsar and to induce him to alleviate the prisoner's lot, and this motive is apparent in many of its pages. Bakunin was not part of some revolutionary movement—he felt isolated and alone, and had suffered much in the past two years. Three years later still in prison, he was to write to his sister Tadyana, "You will never understand what it means to feel yourself buried alive, to say to yourself at every moment of day and night; I am a slave, I am annihilated, reduced to lifelong impotence."[1]

Bakunin was keen to gain the sympathy of the Tsar and thus ameliorate his stifling conditions, for, as Guillaume records, Bakunin feared that prison life would break his spirit. It never did, but there is much in the confession that could hardly have endeared him to the Tsar. It gives a full account of his revolutionary activities from the time he left Russia in 1840 until he was arrested in Dresden; it praises the revolutionary zeal of the French workers during the 1848 uprising; it bewails the fact that Russia is a land of greater oppression than any other in Europe; and it deliberately fails to implicate or name any of his associates. What comes out strongly in the confession is an almost paranoid dislike of Germany for their oppression of the Slavs and the fervent advocacy of the liberation of the Slav peoples. It expressed, as Carr puts it, a "flaming Slav patriotism."[2] Bakunin's hopes for Russia were stated in the following significant paragraph:

> In Russia I wanted a republic, but what kind of republic? Not a parliamentary one! I believe that in Russia more than anywhere else, a strong dictatorial power will be indispensable, but one which would concern itself solely with raising the standard of living and education of the peasant masses; a power free in direction and spirit but without parliamentary privileges; free to print books expressing the ideas of the people, hallowed by their Soviets, strengthened by their free activity, and unconstricted by anything or anyone.[3]

At this time, Bakunin still unconsciously saw the Tsar as a "father-figure" who would paradoxically establish, through a dictatorship, a free peasant-based social order. The document ends with two pleas: one, that he should be allowed to transfer from prison to Siberia, not left "to rot for ever in confinement in a fortress," and the other, that he be allowed to visit his family—whom he had not heard from since 1845—before going into exile. The Tsar was seemingly unmoved by the confession and left Bakunin to rot in jail—though he sanctioned visits from his family.

Bakunin was to spend almost three years in the Peter and Paul fortress, renowned throughout the nineteenth century for its dark, damp, and insanitary conditions. Solitary confinement must have been particularly difficult for a sociable and exuberant person like Bakunin to endure. His health began to deteriorate, mainly because of the atrocious prison diet. He suffered from piles and scurvy, aggravated by the fact that there was almost a total lack of movement. He suffered continuous headaches and shortness of breath, and his teeth began to fall out.[4] In March 1854, Bakunin was transferred to Schlusselberg prison on the shores of Lake Ladoga. In December of that year, Bakunin's father died, at the age of eighty-eight, totally enfeebled and completely blind. Two months later, Tsar Nicholas I himself died and Bakunin's circumstances were completely transformed, for his mother after forty-five years of marriage, and then aged sixty-two, became an entirely new person. Bakunin had never been very fond of his mother, but all of a sudden she began campaigning for her son's release. She petitioned those close to the new Tsar, stressing that her other five sons had served loyally in the Tsar's army. Eventually in February 1857, Bakunin was granted permission to address a petition to the Tsar, and a few weeks later he was informed that Alexander II had given him the choice of staying in prison or going into permanent exile in Siberia. Bakunin chose the latter. It was paradoxical, Carr writes, that Bakunin should "have owed his liberation at last to the mother whom he had never loved, and who had perhaps felt for him in his youth less than the normal measure of maternal affection."[5]

After spending a short time with his family at Premukhino, which he had not seen for almost seventeen years, Bakunin went into exile in Siberia, and compared with those in prison they were to be happy, carefree years. The first months were a period of physical and moral recuperation. He settled at Tomsk, and to supplement his income he began teaching French to the two daughters of a Polish merchant named Kwiatkowski. He became very fond of one of the daughters, Antonia, then eighteen years of age. He proposed marriage to her, and was accepted. They were married in the late summer of 1858; Bakunin was then forty-four years of age. It was a strange match; one of convenience rather than love, though a strong bond of affection held them together throughout their lives. Bakunin during his early manhood had been loved by many women, and he formed close and intimate relationships with several of them. But such relationships were invariably of a "spiritual" kind, for the evidence suggests that Bakunin was sexually impotent. His amazing energy, both physical and mental, has been seen as related to his sexual sterility.[6] It was probably the need for companionship, after the long years of isolation, that prompted Bakunin to seek marriage. In the spring of 1859 Bakunin and his wife obtained permission to move to Irkutsk, and he obtained a post—at a salary of 2,000 rubles a year—with a trading company. This enabled him to travel freely around eastern Siberia. He became friendly with the governor of the territory, Nicholas Muraviev, a second cousin, and began to make plans (as his correspondence with Herzen indicates) for the emancipation of the Slavs through a "rational dictatorship." He was, at this time, as Nettlau writes, filled with a "national psychosis."[7]

Bakunin, however, was growing increasingly dissatisfied with his situation in Siberia, and he decided to make his escape. In June 1861, having obtained advances from some Siberian merchants and letters of introduction to the captains of ships sailing on the Amur, Bakunin said farewell to his wife, and made his way down to the mouth of the River Adur. He took a ship to the southern port of Kastri, and then managed to transfer to an American sailing vessel trading with Japanese ports. At the end of August he arrived in Yokohama. He travelled via San Francisco and New York to Liverpool, arriving there on December 27, 1861. He immediately went to London and was greeted by Herzen and Ogarev as a long-lost brother.

NOTES

1. Carr, E. H. 1937. *Michael Bakunin*, New York: Knopf, p. 232.
2. Carr, op. cit., p. 223.
3. Dolgoff, S., ed., trans, introd., 1973. *Bakunin on Anarchy*, New York: Knopf, p. 70.
4. Carr, op. cit., p. 231.
5. Ibid., p. 234.
6. Masters, A. 1974. *Bakunin: The Father of Anarchism*, London: Sidgwich and Jackson, p. 25.
7. Maximoff, G. P., ed., 1953. *The Political Philosophy of Bakunin: Scientific Anarchism*. Glencoe: Free Press, p. 42.

Chapter 4

From Pan-Slavism to Anarchism

BAKUNIN arrived in London, as Carr puts it, "like a ghost from the past. He was like a man awakened from a long trance."[1] While he had been away—in prison and in exile for more than a decade—much had happened. The revolution had collapsed and reaction had set in throughout Europe. The European reaction, wrote Herzen, "did not exist for Bakunin, the bitter years from 1848 to 1858 did not exist for him either."[2] Bakunin was eager to continue where he had left off—in revolutionary activity. Physically Bakunin had changed a lot. He was now forty-eight, but the years in prison had aged him. He was even more bulky, weighing about 280 pounds, and stood six foot four, immense in those days. He had lost all his teeth and his hair and beard were of a luxuriant growth. Marx said he looked like a bullock. Herzen had also aged during the fourteen years since they had last met. His life, moreover, had been one of tragedy. His wife had died in childbirth, after a long and complicated love affair with Herwegh. And he had become increasingly disillusioned with the triumph of reaction. But though Bakunin had aged physically, he was still full of revolutionary zeal. "Imprisonment, if it had broken the body, had not tamed his incorrigible optimism," his biographer writes.[3] He set about trying to revolutionize Herzen's journal *Kolokol (The Bell)*, arguing that propaganda was not sufficient and that immediate action should be generated. He advocated the formation of revolutionary organizations. He made up for his years of silence and solitude, Herzen wrote, "he argued, lectured, made arrangements, shouted, decided, directed, organized and encouraged all day long, all night long for days and nights together."[4] Bakunin wrote to his friend George Sand in Paris that he still felt young, and that "cut off from political life for thirteen years, I am thirsting for action and consider that, next to life, action is the highest form of happiness."[5]

During the short period that Bakunin spent in London he took little interest in English politics or in the emerging trade union movement, for he was then preoccupied with the possibilities of instigating revolution in eastern Europe. He was still, as Carr notes, "the mercurial and visionary apostle of universal revolution."[6] He was still occupied with the idea of setting up a network of secret societies, not only throughout Bohemia, but in Russia as well. He expressed a continuing enthusiasm for Pan-Slavism, for the establishment of a free-Slav federation that would trigger a revolution throughout Europe. This Pan-Slavism went hand-in-hand with a fervent hatred of the Germans, as he indicated in letters to his sister-in-law, Natalie Bakunin. But Nettlau stresses that deeply buried beneath this nationalist psychosis, an inherent socialism could also be discerned, and that this was evident in two important articles that Bakunin wrote while in London.

The first was published as a supplement to *The Bell*, and was written in the form of an "open letter" entitled "To My Russian, Polish and other Slav Friends." It appeared in February 1862, and established Bakunin as one of the precursors of Russian populism. A significant paragraph advises university students to "go to the people," a phrase which was to become the watchword for the Narodniks.

> So young friends, leave this dying world—these universities, academies and schools in which you are now locked, and where you are permanently separated from the people. Go to the people. This is your field, your life, your science. Learn from the people how best to serve their cause! Remember, friends, that educated youth must be neither the teacher, the paternalistic benefactor, nor the dictatorial leader of the people, but only the midwife for the self-liberation, inspiring them to increase their power by acting together and co-ordinating their efforts.[7]

He argues that the nobility must give the people the land and full freedom, and that the only living force must be the people—the peasants and workers.

The second article is entitled "The People's Cause: Romanov, Pugahev or Pestel?," which was grudgingly published by Herzen in *The Bell* in 1862. It reflects the influence of a young peasant revolutionary whom Bakunin had met in the autumn of 1861—Peter Martyanov. Energetic and deeply emotional, Martyanov had great faith in the Tsar, whom he implored to free the Russian people from the aristocracy and upper classes. He wrote a pamphlet entitled "The People and the State" (1862), which Carr suggests anticipates some of Bakunin's later anarchist ideas. Martyanov returned to Russia the following year, was arrested and condemned to five years hard labour in Siberia. He died there in 1866. Herzen described Martyanov as a "rebel Spartacus."

The three alternatives mentioned in Bakunin's own pamphlet refer to three potential leaders of the revolution, and thus to different kinds of revolution—a peasant uprising such as that led by Emelyan Pugachev in the eighteenth century; a revolution led by the intelligentsia such as the Decembrist revolt of 1825 led by Pavel Pestell, or a peaceful revolution "from above" led by the Tsar, Alexander II. Bakunin seems to have settled for a revolutionary dictatorship by the Romanov—he had suggested a similar scenario to Nicholas I in his confession. He thought that the Tsar was capable of really working with the people, and the people capable of imposing its will on the Tsar through a national assembly.[8] What Bakunin wasn't very keen on was a revolution led by the bourgeois intelligentsia and the setting up of a constitutional monarchy. But as Carr writes, Bakunin's conception of a revolutionary dictator was then still "obscure and ill-defined."[9] Ogarev and Herzen found all this very confusing, and Herzen was even more perturbed by Bakunin's ardent support for the insurrectionary movement that had erupted in Russia; during the summer of 1861, young radicals in St. Petersburg had formed a secret society known as Zemlya I Volya (Land and Liberty). The name was taken from an article by Ogarev in *The Bell* which began "What do the people need? It is very simple. The people need Land and Liberty."[10] The principal organizer of Land and Liberty was Nicholas Serno-Solovievich. As to be expected, Bakunin enthusiastically embraced the cause of Land and Liberty, and urged Herzen to support the society through the pages of *The Bell*. But although Herzen had been attacked as one of the instigators of the revolutionary nihilism that was spreading throughout Russia, he himself was a moderate liberal and was disturbed by their activities. Bakunin and Herzen thus became more and more estranged from one another. George Woodcock notes their underlying differences even before the schism over Land and Liberty:

> Differences of personality and opinion soon divided them. Herzen in his own way was near to the anarchism which Bakunin was now approaching; he detested the State, despised Western democracies, and saw the salvation of Europe in the Russian peasant and his communal way of living. But he had not Bakunin's burning faith in violence and destruction, and temperamentally he was too pessimistic to expect anything more revolutionary in Russia than a constitutional government. He also distrusted the Poles and their brand of expansive

nationalism. Consequently, the partnership lasted uneasily for a few months, and then Bakunin withdrew to concentrate on his own grandiose plans.[11]

Such plans became focused around the Polish insurrection of 1863, which had long been imminent. Like Herzen, Bakunin was deeply committed to the cause of Polish independence. When he was in Brussels in 1844, Bakunin had met the Polish historian and patriot, Joachim Lelewel, who had participated in the Polish insurrection of 1831. This meeting as Nomad wrote, marks the beginning of that period of Bakunin's life when his activities and his thoughts were devoted to the cause of the democratic emancipation of the Slavic people.[12] And as we have noted, Bakunin participated in the Slav congress held in Prague in June 1848. When the Polish insurrection broke out early in 1863—provoked by the Russian authorities who had ordered conscription for the Russian army in Poland—Bakunin immediately became involved in the independence struggle. He wrote letters to the national Committee, offering to stir up peasant revolts in the Ukraine and Lithuania. While Herzen was sceptical of Polish prospects, Bakunin was full of enthusiasm. Plans were made to organize a Russian legion that would support the insurrection and, in February 1863, Bakunin went to Stockholm (where he was reunited with his wife Antonia) in order to get help from Sweden. There Bakunin was acclaimed as the famous Russian revolutionary, and in May a banquet was organized in his honour by a number of Swedish radicals. But the Polish legion's plans under Colonel Lapinski, of invading Poland from the Baltic, ended in fiasco, and the Polish insurrection itself was crushed by Russian troops. Bakunin thus found himself stranded in Sweden, and highly disillusioned with the cause of the revolutionary nationalism. It was clear to him that many Polish nationalists were more concerned with territorial expansion—laying claims to the Ukraine—than with Polish national freedom, and that they were fearful of a peasant uprising in Poland (and in Russia itself), which they viewed as more terrible than the continuation of Tsarist rule. Meanwhile, the Land and Liberty movement had been suppressed in Russia where political reaction was again at the forefront. Because Herzen, through his periodical *The Bell*, had supported both the Polish cause and the Land and Liberty, he was now branded as a traitor and a friend of terrorists. Circulation of *The Bell* slumped from around 3,000 in 1861 to 500 two years later. Thus, *The Bell* which had been widely read in Russia as the voice of progressive liberalism was now seen as little more than a propaganda sheet for terrorists. Herzen unfairly blamed this change of fortune on Bakunin, and their relationship became further strained. It was never again to be close. Bakunin admired Herzen as a political journalist, and as a "writer of genius," but, he wrote, "he decidedly has not in him the stuff of which revolutionary leaders are made."[13]

Bakunin thus decided to leave London and move to Italy. But in November 1864 he paid a short visit to London and there met Karl Marx. It was their first meeting in sixteen years and it was to be the last face-to-face encounter. It was Marx who asked to see Bakunin hoping to re-establish friendly relations with Bakunin and to invite him to support the newly-formed International Workingmen's Association (usually known as the First International). In 1862 an exhibition of modern industry was held in London. A number of French workers came to see the exhibition and began to have discussions with English trade union members. They decided to form an organization, the International Workingmen's Association, which was formally inaugurated in September 1864—though its structure and its constitution were not formally adopted until the first congress convened in Geneva in September 1866. It began primarily, as G. D. H. Cole notes, as a "trade union affair," though trade unions were then still illegal in France. Most of the French participants in the 1864 proceedings—Tolain, Limousin, Varlin—were not industrial workers but artisans, and essentially followers of Proudhon's kind of socialism. Hence, the First International began as a joint affair between British and French trade unionists with the participation of a number of exiles from other parts of Europe. Karl Marx was the most important of these, and because of his academic stature— he liked to be called "Herr Doctor"—he quickly became one of its most important and active leaders. Its essential aim was the building up of "a vigorous trade union movement, of taking independent working class political action, and of emphasizing the separation of the workers from the revolutionary radicalism both of the bourgeoisie and the followers of August Blanqui, between whom and the Proudhonists (Proudhon died in 1865) the conscious elements among the French workers divided their allegiance."[14] The First International was therefore not the creation of Marx, nor was it specifically Marxist at its inception. When Bakunin visited Marx, the latter scholar was, as a leading committee member, involved in drafting the rules and the inaugural manifesto of the association. Bakunin apparently made a good impression on Marx. "I must say," wrote Marx to his friend Engels, (November 4, 1864), "that I liked him very much—better than before." Marx was not immune from Bakunin's personal magnetism. Marx continued:

Bakunin wished to be remembered to you. He has left for Italy today. I saw him yesterday evening once more, for the first time after sixteen years. He said that after the failure of Poland he should, in future, confine himself, to participation in the socialist movement. On the whole he is one of the few persons whom I find not to have retrogressed after sixteen years, but to have developed further.[15]

Bakunin himself described the interview in the following terms:

At that time I had a little note from Marx, in which he asked me whether he could come to see me the next day. I answered in the affirmative, and he came. He had an explanation. He said that he had never said or done anything against me; that, on the contrary, he had always been my true friend, and had great respect for me. I knew that he was lying, but I really no longer bear any grudge against him. The renewal of the acquaintanceship interested me moreover in another connection. I knew that he had taken a great part in the foundation of the International. I had read the manifesto written by him in the name of the provisional General Council, a manifesto that came from his pen when he was not engaged in personal polemic. In a word, we parted, outwardly on the best of terms, although I did not return his visit.[16]

Bakunin had a profound respect for Marx's intellectual abilities and for his contributions to the revolutionary cause, and even considered himself a "pupil" of Marx. But although at their reunion in 1864 Marx invited Bakunin to join the International, he refused, preferring to go to Italy to devote himself to organizing secret societies. Guillaume suggests that Bakunin's decision was understandable, for at that time, the International, outside the General Council in London and a few mutualist (i.e. Proudhonist) workers from Paris, could hardly be termed an International organization, and no one could then foresee its later importance.[17]

Bakunin lived in Italy from 1864 to 1867, living first in Florence, then in and around Naples. It was during this period that he finally rejected nationalism and formulated his doctrine of revolutionary socialism. While in Italy, he met the legendary figure of Italian revolutionary nationalism, Giuseppe Garibaldi, and Elie and Elisée Reclus, who were later to have an important influence on the anarchist movement.[18] In Florence, Bakunin gathered around him a group of dissatisfied Italian radicals, particularly those who had become disillusioned with Mazzini's style of republican nationalism. He also renewed his interest in Freemasonry, which, with its stress on secrecy and ritual, had a strong appeal to Bakunin. But in that period, Freemasonry had a radical and progressive import, and it is suggested that it had an important influence on Bakunin's religious beliefs. In his early years, Bakunin had been hostile to the theory and practice of orthodox Christianity, but had by no means abandoned them. He often stressed his own personal belief in God and, in 1849, in Hegelian fashion and under the influence of Feuerbach, he had written:

> You are mistaken if you think that I do not believe in God.
> I seek God in man, in human freedom and now I seek God in revolution.[19]

His contact with Freemasonry—and with Proudhon—heralded a radical change in his thought, and he became a fervent atheist. He was then fifty years of age.

After spending the happy summer of 1865 in Sorrento with Antonia, and with his brother Paul and his wife Natalie, Bakunin moved in October to Naples. There he met and enjoyed the patronage of an eccentric high-ranking Russian aristocrat—the Princess Obolensky. Living apart from her husband, and in opulent splendour, the Princess supported all kinds of radicals and revolutionaries who gathered around her "like bees round a honey jar."[20] Bakunin took advantage of her generosity towards radicals. As in Florence, Bakunin began to organize around him a group of supporters, mostly Italian, but including also some Polish and Russian radicals. It constituted itself as a secret organization, the Fraternité Internationale (the International Brotherhood). Bakunin wrote out, in French, the aims and principles of this secret society, which became known as the "Revolutionary Catechism" (1866), which is not to be confused with the "Catechism of the Revolutionist" which was essentially written by Sergei Nechaev, and which is very different in both style and content. Although, as we have suggested, Bakunin had an inherent predilection for secret societies, it must be noted that when political dissent is outlawed—as it was in most European countries during the nineteenth century—the revolutionaries are forced to organize secret societies. Bakunin was not alone in this, for as Dolgoff writes "almost everyone conspired—the Poles, the Italians, the Russians, the Blanquists, and the nascent unions camouflaged as 'social clubs'."[21] Bakunin was convinced that the International Fraternity, as a kind of vanguard society, was essential for the success of the revolutionary movement. The "Revolutionary Catechism" is primarily concerned with outlining, for the benefit of the members of the Fraternity, a practical programme of action with respect to the coming revolution. It indicates Bakunin's renunciation of radical nationalism, and the first outline of his anarchist creed. The document has been described as being the "spiritual foundation of the entire anarchist movement." Max Nomad writes that it was "the secret gospel of the first courageous apostles of modern anarchism."[22] It would be useful to quote some of the more important paragraphs of the "Revolutionary Catechism":

II. In replacing the cult of God by respect and love for humanity, we proclaim human reason as the only criteria of truth; human conscience as the basis of justice; individual and collective freedom as the only source of order in society.

III. Freedom is the absolute right of every adult man and woman to seek no other sanction for their acts than their own conscience and their own reason, being responsible first for themselves and then to the society which they have voluntarily accepted.

IX. Political Organization. It is impossible to determine a concrete universal and obligatory norm for the internal development and political organization of every nation. The life of each nation is subordinated to a plethora of different historical, geographical, and economic conditions, making it impossible to establish a model of organization equally valid for all. However, without certain absolutely essential conditions the practical realization of freedom will be forever impossible. These conditions are:
A. The abolition of all State religions and all privileged churches.
C. Abolition of monarchy; establishment of a commonwealth.

D. Abolition of classes, ranks and privileges; absolute equality of political rights for all men and women; universal suffrage.

E. Abolition and economic dismantling of the all-pervasive, regimented, centralized State . . . and all State institutions. Abolition of all centralized administration, of the bureaucracy, of all permanent armies and State police.

F. Immediate direct election of all judicial and civil functionaries as well as representatives (national, provincial, and communal delegates) by the universal suffrage of both sexes.

G. The internal reorganization of each country on the basis of the absolute freedom of individuals, of the production associations, and of the communes.

H. Individual rights.

1. The right of every man and woman, from birth to adulthood, to complete upkeep, clothes, food, shelter, care, guidance, education . . . all at the expense of society.

3. The freedom of adults of both sexes must be absolute and complete, freedom to come and go, to voice all opinions, to be lazy or active, moral or immoral, in short, to dispose of one's persons or possessions as one pleases, being accountable to no one.

K. The basic unit of all political organization in each country must be the completely autonomous commune, constitution by the majority vote of all adults of both sexes.

L. The province must be nothing but a free federation of autonomous communes.

M. The nation must be nothing but a federation of autonomous provinces.

X. Special Organization. Without political equality there can be no real political liberty, but political equality will be possible only when there is social and economic equality.

A. Equality does not imply the levelling of individual differences. Diversity in capacities and powers—those differences between races, nations, sexes, ages and persons—far from being a social evil, constitutes, on the contrary, the abundance of humanity.

D. Abolition of the right of inheritance.

H. Labour being the sole source of wealth, everyone is free to die of hunger or to live in the deserts or the forests . . . but whoever wants to live in society must earn his living by his own labour.

L. The land, and all natural resources, are the common property of everyone, but will be used only by those who cultivate it by their own labour.

O. From the moment of pregnancy to birth, a woman and her children shall be subsidized by the communal organizations.

Q. Children belong neither to their parents nor to society. They belong to themselves and to their own future liberty.

T. The old, sick and infirm will enjoy all political and social rights and be bountifully supported at the expense of society.[23]

The "Revolutionary Catechism" outlines an essentially anarchist doctrine—libertarian, atheistic, socialist and anti-State. Nomad regarded it as a "camouflaged form of decentralized democracy."[24] It indicates the combined ideas and influences of Proudhon and Marx. To bring about this revolution Bakunin advocates a secret society. He writes that in order to prepare for this revolution it will be necessary to conspire and to organize a strong secret association co-ordinated by an international nucleus.[25]

But strangely, in outlining the organizational structure within this secret association, Bakunin advocates a hierarchical structure and almost unlibertarian stress on internal discipline and on obedience to the national juntas. Thus, Max Nomad concludes that "obedience, discipline, subordination, constitute the leitmotif of this famous classic of Anarchism.[26] Yet Bakunin makes it clear that this secret organization in no sense constitutes a revolutionary dictatorship; the "rigorous discipline" is in the interests of the cause, and the "single will" to be obeyed, is that of the principles of the organization.[27]

The revolution, he writes, can only triumph if a political or national revolution is transformed into a socialist revolution, and this can only be achieved by, and under the direction of, working people. The Secret International fraternity "has its origin in the conviction that revolutions are never made by individuals or even by secret societies. They make themselves; they are produced by the force of circumstances, the movement of facts and events. They receive a long preparation in the deep, instinctive consciousness of the masses."[28] The revolutionaries constituting the secret fraternity act as "midwives" to the revolution; they are neither separate from, nor do they have direction over the revolution. "The revolution must be made not for but by the people and can never succeed if it does not enthusiastically involve all the masses of the people, that is, in the rural countryside as well as in the cities."[29] We shall return to Bakunin's conception of revolution and the role of secret societies later in this study.

During their stay in Italy, Bakunin's wife Antonia—whom he affectionately called Tonia—became emotionally involved with one of Bakunin's close associates in the International Brotherhood, Carlo Gambuzzi. Unable to consummate his marriage with Antonia, Bakunin seems to have been quite unaffected by this love affair. He tolerated it, and cared for the two children born of the liaison. In August 1867, Bakunin left Italy and went to Geneva to attend a large conference that had been convened there. An invitation to the conference had been extended to "all friends of free democracy," and among its supporters were John Bright and John Stuart Mill in England, Garibaldi in Italy, Louis Blanc and Victor Hugo in France, as well as the Russians, Herzen and Ogarev, both of whom had moved to Geneva. Around 6,000 people attended the congress, its support coming mainly from France and Germany, and from Geneva itself. It was, as Carr described it, "a predominantly bourgeois affair—liberal and pacifist in complexion, but certainly not revolutionary."[30] Bakunin had no illusions about the organization, but he was welcomed to the congress with great acclaim. A young Russian positivist who attended the congress described the occasion:

> ... with a heavy awkward gait he mounted the steps leading to the platform where the Bureau (the executive committee) sat, dressed as carelessly as ever in a sort of grey blouse, beneath which was visible not a shirt but a flannel vest, the cry passed from mouth to mouth: "Bakunin!" Garibaldi, who was in the chair, stood up, advanced a few steps and embraced him. This solemn meeting of two old and tried warriors of revolution produced an astonishing impression ... Everyone rose, and there was a prolonged and enthusiastic clapping of hands.[31]

The conference had been held to discuss the possibilities of peace in Europe and to establish the United States of Europe. On the second day of the congress Bakunin addressed the delegates in a speech that won prolonged applause. Besides denouncing the Russian Empire, of which he said he was "the most disobedient subject," Bakunin declared that it could only be saved by a combination of federalism and socialism. He attacked nationalism (which he earlier linked with the revolution) suggesting that it was inevitably the tool of reaction. The main thrust of his speech was the need to establish a federal political system. Universal peace, he is reported to have said "will be impossible as long as the present centralized States exist. We must desire their destruction in order that, on the ruins of these forced unions organized from above by right of authority and conquest, there may arise free unions organized from below by the free federation of communes into provinces, of provinces into the nation, and of nations into the United States of Europe."[32]

The congress voted—amid rising disagreements—to establish a League of Peace and Freedom which would hold annual congresses. Bakunin became a member of its central committee. Throughout the following year, Bakunin devoted himself energetically to League activities in an attempt to induce the committee to adopt a social revolutionary programme. He wrote a long document entitled "Federalism, Socialism and Anti-Theologism," which bore the subtitle "Reasoned Proposal to the Central Committee of the League for Peace and Freedom, by M. Bakunin. Geneva." Much of the paper is devoted to a denunciation of religion—for Garibaldi himself at the Geneva congress had, in the opening speech, begged the delegates "to adopt the religion of God." Yet, although written in haste and with enthusiasm, "Federalism, Socialism and Anti-Theologism" is an important theoretical work, for it outlines cogently many of Bakunin's basic ideas—a critique of nationalism; the advocacy of a revolutionary socialism that is distinct from the authoritarian or State socialism of the utopian socialists such as Saint Simon and Cabet; the outline of a federalist political system which denies "the historic right of the State." In a critique of Rousseau, Bakunin also introduces the critical distinction between society and the State—which Rousseau had virtually conflated—and stresses, long before Lord Acton, the corrupting influence of power. It is of interest that in his critique of the Jacobin or "doctrinaire" form of socialism, Bakunin does not in fact mention Marx, although many of Marx's ideas permeate the text.

Bakunin managed to convince the central committee of the League to accept his proposals. Consequently, the programme adopted for the

Berne congress in September clearly bore the imprint of Bakunin's ideas. Its substantive paragraphs ran as follows:

> The League recognizes that it is absolutely essential not to separate three fundamental aspects of the social problem; the religious question, the political question and the economic question. It therefore affirms:

(1) that religion, being a matter for the individual conscience, must be eliminated from political institutions and from the domain of public instruction in order that the churches may not be able to fetter the free development of society;

(2) that the United States of Europe cannot be organized in any other form than that of popular institution united by means of federation and having as their basis the principle and equality of personal rights and the autonomy of communes and provinces in the regulation of their own interests;

(3) that the present economic system requires radical change if we wish to achieve that equitable division of wealth, labour, leisure and education which is a fundamental condition of the liberation of the working classes and the elimination of the proletariat.[33]

However, at the second congress of the League of Peace and Freedom, held on September 18, 1867, this programme was voted down after a heated debate. Bakunin, therefore, along with the minority faction of revolutionary socialists, founded on the same day a new, open—not secret—organization called the International Alliance of Socialist Democracy. Bakunin wrote the Alliance's Declaration of Principles. Among other things, it stated that:

> The Alliance declares itself atheist; it seeks the complete and definitive abolition of classes and the political, economic and social equality of both sexes. It wants the land and the instruments of labour (production), like all other property, to be converted into the collective property of the whole society for the utilization by the workers; that is, by agricultural and industrial associations. It affirms that all the existing political and authoritarian States, which are to be reduced to simple administrative utilities in their respective countries, must eventually be replaced by a worldwide union of free association, agricultural and industrial.[34]

In July 1868, Bakunin had become a member of the Geneva section of the International Working Men's Association—and many of his associates were already members. He therefore proposed an alliance between the International and the newly formed International Alliance of Socialist Democracy. Through an intermediary, Johann Becker, a friend of Marx and a veteran of the 1848 revolution, Marx was approached with the following proposals—that alliance members, while being members of the International, should equally be allowed to hold their own meetings, and that the various branches of the alliance, while keeping their autonomy, should become members of the International as well.[35]

The Brussels congress of the International which met in early September had already distanced itself from the League of Peace and Freedom; it was therefore inevitable that when the Alliance formally applied for membership of the International it was rejected by the General Council in London. The latter declared, in December 1868, that "the presence of a second international body operating inside or outside the International Workingmen's Association would be the surest means of disorganizing the latter."[36] Bakunin had clearly seen the Alliance as an anarchist group within the Association, enjoying a certain autonomy and "acting as a kind of radical ginger group."[37] But he accepted the decision of the General Council and in response to an inquiry about his doings, Bakunin wrote a warm, personal letter to Marx (December 22, 1868), in which he remarked:

> I have come to understand better than ever how right you were when you followed, and invited us all to follow, the great high road of economic revolution, and abused those of us who were losing themselves on the by-roads of national, or purely political, adventures. I am doing now what you began to do twenty years ago. Since bidding a solemn and public farewell to the bourgeois at the Berne congress, I have known no other company, no other work than that of the workers. My country is now the International.[38]

The Alliance was publicly dissolved and, in March 1869, the International Fraternity was also disbanded. The local group in Geneva, Bakunin and his associates, then became simply a section of the International. Carr intimates that a "wooden horse had entered the Trojan citadel."[39] Yet at the very moment that Bakunin was publicly announcing his allegiance to the International, he was also beginning to articulate—for the first time—the basic principles of anarchism which he was to propagate for the remaining years of his life, and to clearly differentiate his own brand of socialism from that of Marx. In a speech to the League of Peace and Freedom in September 1868, Bakunin had denied that he was a communist. I hate communism, he said:

> . . . because it is the negation of liberty and because humanity is for me unthinkable without liberty. I am not a communist, because communism concentrates and swallows up in itself for the benefit of the State all the forces of society, because it inevitably leads to the concentration of property in the hands of the State, whereas I want the abolition of the State, the final eradication of the principle of authority . . . I want to see society and collective or social property organized from below upward by way of free association, not from above downwards, by means of any kind of authority whatever . . . I am a collectivist, but not a communist.[40]

In January 1869, representatives of the thirty sections of the International in French Switzerland met in Geneva for the purpose of founding a local federation. It was called the Federation Romande, and it established *L'Égalité*, written in a popular style to appeal to the workers. Bakunin wrote several articles for *L'Égalité*, stressing the need for revolutionary socialists to distance themselves from all forms of bourgeois politics. He stressed the crucial importance of the ideas contained in the statutes of the International, namely that "the emancipation of the workers is the task of the workers themselves."[41] It was through the Federation Romande that Bakunin became friendly with the young school-teacher James Guillaume, whom he had met at the first congress of the League for Peace and Freedom in 1867. Guillaume, Carr writes, "possessed both the virtues and the limitations of the frugal mountaineer," for Guillaume came from the small town of Le Locle in the Jura mountains. A keen intellect and an excellent administrator, Guillaume was to become a close associate and disciple of Bakunin, and an important chronicler of the First International.

In September 1869, Bakunin attended the fourth congress of the International, which was held in Basel. Marx, as usual, did not attend. Around seventy-five delegates came to the congress, but only a small group could be called devotees of Bakunin. But among his supporters, besides Guillaume, were Albert Richard from Lyons, Caesar Paepe, a doctor from Belgium and Eugène Varlin, a bookbinder and left-wing Proudhonist from Paris. Varlin was killed in 1871 by reactionaries after the fall of the Paris commune. Bakunin was a dominant influence at the Basel conference, not because he carried the greatest number of votes, but because of the persuasiveness of his personality. In a debate on the abolition of private property, Bakunin delivered a long and brilliant speech advocating its abolition, as well as demanding that of the State "which is the only guarantee of existing property." On this issue there was no serious disagreement between Bakunin and the German Marxists, and, as many have stressed, it marked the defeat of the Proudhonists who still clung to small-scale property. In the debate on the eradication of inheritance, Bakunin, for whom this proposal was a kind of obsession, again spoke eloquently demanding its "complete and radical abolition." This was a proposal that Marx found completely illogical. He wrote to his son-in-law Paul Lafargue that Bakunin was a charlatan and an ignoramus. It is evident, Marx noted:

> If you have had the power to make the social revolution in one day . . . you would abolish at once landed property and capital, and would therefore have no occasion at all to occupy yourselves with le *droit d'héritage*. On the other hand, if you have not that power . . . the proclamation of the abolition of inheritance would not be a serious act, but a foolish menace, rallying the whole peasantry and the whole small middle-class round reaction.[42]

Marx argued that the economy was the basis of jurisprudence and that inheritance laws were the effect and not the cause of a social organization based on private property. He is even more scathing of Bakunin's use of the phrase "the equality of different classes." This blunder, he wrote to Lafargue, shows you the shameless ignorance and superficiality of Bakunin, a "Mahomet without a Koran"—although it is clear that Bakunin meant by this phrase an equitable division of wealth not the maintenance of a class structure. But even more aggravating to Marx and Engels was the fact that the Basel congress rejected by a large majority the resolution endorsing the report of the General Council. It was evident that Marx was no longer in supreme command of the International, and that he had to contend with a serious rival for the control and direction of the organization. From this point on, the struggle between Marx and Bakunin deepened. It was evident also that the delegates to the Basel congress were divided into two distinct ideological groups. On the one hand, there were the State socialists—the English trade unionists, the German Marxists and the followers of Auguste Blanqui; on the other, were the libertarian socialists who took the name "collectivists." They were largely followers of Bakunin and came primarily from France, Spain, Italy and the Swiss Alps. Thus, although the conflict between Marx and Bakunin was focused around disputes within the International, it is important to stress that it was also a conflict of personalities, and of fundamentally different conceptions of socialism.

NOTES

1. Carr, E. H. 1937. *Michael Bakunin*, New York: Knopf, p. 252.
2. Masters, A. 1974. *Bakunin: The Father of Anarchism*, London: Sidgwich and Jackson, p. 135.
3. Carr, op. cit., p. 252.
4. Masters, op. cit., p. 137.
5. Carr, op. cit., p. 252.
6. Carr, op. cit., p. 258.
7. Dolgoff, S. ed., trans., introd., 1973. *Bakunin on Anarchy*, New York: Knopf, p. 388.
8. Venturi, F. 1960. *Roots of Revolution; A History of Populist & Socialist Movements in 19th Century Russia*, Trans. F. Haskell, University of Chicago Press, p. 111.
9. Carr, op. cit., p. 278.
10. Carr, op. cit., pp. 279-80.
11. Woodcock, G. 1962. *Anarchism*. Harmondsworth: Penguin, p. 147.
12. Nomad, M. 1933. *Apostles of Revolution*. New York: Collier, p. 155.
13. Carr, op. cit., p. 312.
14. Cole, G.D.H., 1954. *History of Socialist Thought, Vol. II, Marxism and Anarchism 1850-1890*. London: Macmillan, pp. 909-91.
15. Aldred, G. A. 1940. *Bakunin* (pamphlet), 68 pp. Glasgow: Strickland Press, p. 52.
16. Ibid.
17. Dolgoff, op. cit., p. 36.
18. cf. Fleming, M. 1979. *The Anarchist Way to Socialism: Elisée Reclus and 19th Century European Anarchism*. London: Croom Helm.
19. Pyziur, E. 1955. *The Doctrine of Anarchism of Michael Bakunin*, Milwaukee: Regnery, p. 50.
20. Masters, A. 1974. *Bakunin: The Father of Anarchism*, London: Sidgwich and Jackson, p. 165.
21. Dolgoff, op. cit., p. 74.
22. Nomad, op. cit., p. 180.
23. Dolgoff, op. cit., pp. 76-95.
24. Nomad, op. cit., p. 181.
25. Dolgoff, op. cit., p. 101.

26. Nomad, op. cit., p. 183.
27. Lehning, A. 1973. *Michael Bakunin: Selected Writings.* London: Cape, p. 93.
28. Dolgoff, op. cit., p. 155.
29. Dolgoff, op. cit. p. 99.
30. Carr, op. cit., p. 342.
31. Carr, op. cit., p. 343.
32. Carr, op. cit., p. 345.
33. Carr, op. cit., p. 350.
34. Guillaume in Dolgoff, op. cit., p. 35.
35. Masters, op. cit., pp. 180-81.
36. Carr, op. cit., p. 366.
37. Woodcock, op. cit., p. 154.
38. Carr, op. cit., p. 365.
39. Carr, op. cit., p. 374.
40. Carr, op. cit., p. 356.
41. Dolgoff, op. cit., p. 167.
42. April 19, 1870, Marx, K. et al. 1972. *Anarchism and Anarcho-Syndicalism.* Moscow: Progress Publishers, p. 45.

Chapter 5

The Insurrections in France

S HORTLY before the Basel congress, in the summer of 1869, rumours were again circulating that Bakunin was a Russian agent. The main culprits in the spreading of this falsehood were friends of Marx, particularly Wilhelm Liebknecht, a founder of the German Social Democratic party. Feeling persecuted, Bakunin, when he met Liebknecht at the Basel congress, challenged him to substantiate his charges and a "court of honour" was held. Bakunin was publicly exonerated. Liebknecht signed a statement to that effect and shook hands with Bakunin, who then proceeded melodramatically to use the paper to light his cigarette. But the matter did not end there. Another delegate to the congress, Moses Hess, on his return to Paris, wrote a scathing attack on Bakunin accusing him of being a Russophile, an advocate of reactionary Pan-Slavism and secretly trying to undermine the International. The article deeply affected Bakunin and provoked one of his emotional outbursts which revealed a vein of anti-Semitism, that, as Carr writes, "lay deep in the traditions of every Russian aristocrat."[1] But Bakunin's anti-Semitism, as Lampert suggests, was prompted entirely by uncontrolled resentment born of personal feuds with the Marxists, not only with Marx but with Lasalle, Liebknecht, Wetheim and Hess, all of whom, directly or indirectly, spread the slander that Bakunin was "a cunning Russian spy." But before these calumnies began to be disseminated, there was no evidence of Bakunin having anti-Jewish feelings, and even as he denounced Hess and the "crowd of Jewish pygmies," he added, "not Jesus Christ, St. Paul, Spinoza and other great Jewish figures"—not even Marx, for whom he had great respect.[2] Marxists have made much of Bakunin's anti-Semitic sentiments, forgetting that other socialists of the period, including Marx and Engels, were not free of racial stereotypes and prejudices. Marx, as Adam Ulam noted, was himself not entirely free of anti-Semitism.[3] Both Marx and Engels spoke of tribal peoples as "savages" and their abusive and derogatory opinions of peasants, the Swiss and the Slav people are well known. Neither Bakunin nor Marx were immune from the racist and chauvinist sentiments of their day. But interestingly, Bakunin's friend, Alexander Herzen, chided Bakunin for attacking Moses Hess and leaving "Marx the master unchallenged." Herzen, it appears, disliked Marx intensely. In his reply to Herzen, Bakunin wrote (October 1869):

> Why then have I spared him and even praised him as a great man? For two reasons, Herzen. The first is justice. Leaving on one side all his iniquities against us, one cannot help admitting—I, at any rate, cannot—his enormous services to the cause of socialism, which he has served ably, energetically, and faithfully throughout twenty five years since I knew him, and in which he has undoubtedly outstripped us all. He was one of the first founders, almost the chief founder, of the International. That is in my eyes an immense service which I shall always recognize whatever he does against me. The other reason is political calculation, and, in my opinion, perfectly sound tactics . . .
>
> Marx is unquestionably a useful man in the International. He has been hitherto one of the strongest, ablest and most influential supporters of socialism in it, one of the most powerful obstacles to the infiltration into it of any kind of bourgeois tendencies or ideas. I should never forgive myself if, from motives of personal revenge, I destroyed or diminished his undoubtedly beneficial influence. It may happen and probably will happen, that I shall have to enter into conflict with him, not for a personal offence, but on a matter of principle, on a question of State communism, of which he and the party led by him, English and German, are fervent supporters. Then it will be a life and death struggle. But all in good time; the moment has not yet come.[4]

In the spring of 1869 there arrived in Geneva a young Russian student called Sergei Nechaev. The son of a peasant, he had worked as a teacher in St. Petersburg and attended some lectures at the university. There he became involved in revolutionary activities, and when he came to Geneva he was full of revolutionary fervour, with tales of having escaped from the fortress of Peter and Paul as a representative of a vibrant revolutionary movement in Russia. He soon made contact with Bakunin and the two men struck up a rather bizarre friendship. Bakunin was evidently captivated by this young fanatical nihilist, more than thirty years his junior. Together they made plans and formed a

World Revolutionary Alliance with Nechaev designated as Agent No. 271 of the Russian section. This revolutionary organization was, it appears, all a figment of their own imagination, but between April and August 1869 the two men began drafting a series of Russian pamphlets—seven in all. The most famous of these is the "Revolutionary Catechism." A few extracts will suffice to give the tenor of this extraordinary document, which sets forth the rules and duties of members of a non-existent revolutionary secret society.

> The revolutionist is a doomed man. He has no personal interests, no affairs, sentiments, attachments, property, not even a name of his own. Everything in him is absorbed by one exclusive interest, one thought—the revolution . . .
>
> The revolutionist despises every sort of doctrinarianism and has renounced the peaceful scientific pursuits, leaving them to future generations. He knows only one science, the science of destruction . . .
>
> The nature of a real revolutionist precludes every bit of sentimentality, romanticism or infatuation and exchange. It precludes even personal hatred and revenge. Revolutionary passion having become a normal phenomenon, it must be combined with cold calculation . . .
>
> The Association has no aim other than the complete liberation and happiness of the masses, i.e. of the people who live by manual labour . . . the Association therefore does not intend to foist on the people any organization from above. The future organization will no doubt evolve out of the popular movement and out of life itself. But this is the business of future generations. Our business is destruction, terrible, complete, universal and merciless . . .
>
> Let us join with the bold world of bandits—the only genuine revolutionists in Russia.[5]

Another pamphlet "Principles of Revolution" carries the words:

> We recognize no other activity but the work of extermination, but we admit that the forms in which this activity will show itself will be extremely varied—poison, the knife, the rope etc. In this struggle revolution sanctifies everything alike.[6]

There has long been an academic controversy as to whether or not Bakunin was the author of the "Revolutionary Catechism." Infatuated by Nechaev, an ardent pamphleteer, and prone to drafting manifestos of non-existent associations, Bakunin may well have had a hand in the drafting of the document. But recent studies suggest that the "Revolutionary Catechism" was primarily the project of Nechaev alone, and certainly the pamphlet indicates a nihilistic perspective that is fundamentally different from Bakunin's own critique of the existing order. Nechaev was almost pathological in his destructive tendencies, wanting revolution for revolution's sake. In this, as Masters wrote, he went much further than Bakunin, "who still had a tremendous, if naive, faith in humanity and genuinely wanted to bring about a greatly improved life for everyone. Certainly he believed that the existing order must be destroyed but only as a means of creating a new mode of life. Nechaev on the other hand, possessed a ruthless destructiveness that was in no way creative."[7]

Nechaev left for Russia in August 1869, assuring Bakunin that revolution would break out in Russia on February 19 the following year, the ninth anniversary of the liberation of the serfs. He was to spend three months in Russia and while there created a sensation in wilfully murdering, with the connivance of four other revolutionary students, a student named Ivanov. He hurriedly left St. Petersburg and, evading the Russian authorities, reached Switzerland in January 1870. Bakunin immediately invited Nechaev to join him in Locarno, where Bakunin had settled after the Basel congress, finding it cheaper to live in Locarno than in Geneva. Bakunin was now in financial difficulties and to alleviate poverty had agreed to translate Karl Marx's *Das Kapital* into Russian for a St. Petersburg publisher. He had been advanced three hundred rubles for the work, which sufficed to pay his most pressing debts in Geneva. But the translation of Marx's turgid prose proved to be hard-going for Bakunin, who was hardly one to relish such routine scholarly work. He was thus easily persuaded by Nechaev to abandon the translation of the book and to concentrate upon Russian revolutionary propaganda. Nechaev took it upon himself to write a dictatorial letter to Bakunin's publisher, Lyubavin, instructing him, in the name of the central committee of the People's Justice, to leave Bakunin in peace, threatening vengeance otherwise. The letter got into the hands of Marx, who was later to use it to discredit Bakunin, who appears to have had no knowledge at all of Nechaev's letter.

Some attempt was made by Nechaev and Herzen's daughter Natalie, to re-establish the liberal journal *The Bell*, but it was not a success and Bakunin found himself completely cold-shouldered by the scheming and imperious Nechaev. He felt used and duped by the younger man, who meanwhile had managed to extract large amounts of money from Ogarev and the Herzen family. Bakunin himself was imperious by nature and was seldom troubled by scruples—especially over money matters—but as Carr writes, he more than met his match in the unscrupulous Nechaev.[8] In June 1870, Bakunin wrote a long letter to Nechaev, which like all his letters soon developed into a revolutionary pamphlet. In it he reproached Nechaev for his deception and intrigue, for having blackmailed and intimidated Natalie Herzen (whose father had died in January 1870), and for having fallen "so much in love with Jesuit methods that you have forgotten everything else." Neither love nor respect, Bakunin wrote, "can prevent one from telling you frankly that the system of deceit which is increasingly becoming your whole system, your main weapons and means, is fatal to the cause itself."[9] By July 1870, Bakunin had come to realize that Nechaev was simply using him to attain a personal dictatorship by Jesuitical methods, and broke off all relations with the young nihilist. He was very disheartened. Having been separated from Russia for more than thirty years, Nechaev was one of the few serious Russian revolutionaries that Bakunin had met, and he had been completely captivated by his revolutionary zeal. Having created havoc wherever he went, Nechaev fled to London taking with him a suitcase of personal letters which he had stolen—from Bakunin, Ogarev and Natalie Herzen—intent to use them to blackmail their owners in the future if need be. Unlike Nechaev, Bakunin was an amiable person with a generous spirit, and he had clearly been the victim of excessive trustfulness and of his admiration for Nechaev's intense energy. Bakunin confessed to Ogarev in August 1870:

> We have been pretty fine fools. How Herzen would have laughed at us if he were still alive, and how right he would have been! Well, all we can do is to swallow this bitter pill, which will make us more cautious in the future.[10]

Although he was a violent and unscrupulous character, no one can doubt Nechaev's revolutionary fervour or his courage. After residing for a period in London and France, continually trying to evade the authorities, he was eventually captured in Switzerland in August 1872. Taken to Russia, he was confined for ten years in the Peter and Paul fortress in solitary confinement, where he died of scurvy at the age of thirty-five.[11]

In July 1870 the Franco-Prussian war broke out. As it was Napoleon II who declared war, and appeared to be the aggressor, a wave of patriotic feeling swept through Germany. Within about six weeks most of the French armies had been defeated, and on September 1 the imperial force was destroyed at the battle of Sedan, one of the most calamitous defeats of modern times. Three days later a provisional republican government was appointed in Paris. With the collapse of the Empire, France became disorganized and found itself in a constitutional vacuum, without a government having popular support, and with Paris under the immediate threat of occupation. This state of affairs was a tonic to Bakunin's depressed spirit, coinciding as it did with the Nechaev affair. He was immediately gladdened by the news of Napoleon's downfall, but also sensed that the defeat of France by a feudal militarist Germany would effectively mean an end to socialism and the triumph of counterrevolution. But Bakunin also saw another possibility—that the war between France and Prussia might be transformed into a civil war for social revolution. The French people would fight a guerrilla war to repulse the foreign army, while simultaneously defending the revolution against their own discredited rulers. To clarify his ideas Bakunin wrote a long essay entitled "Letters to a Frenchman on the Present Crisis"—the unnamed Frenchman is said to have been Gasard Blanc, one of his followers in Lyons. It was edited and printed by James Guillaume, and thus is one of the clearest and consistent of Bakunin's writings. The letter is about thirty-thousand words in length, and Guillaume divided it into six sections. It calls for the spontaneous uprising of the French people, both workers and peasants, the renunciation of bourgeois politics—including the reformist strategy of the German socialists—and the organization of French society "from the bottom up." He writes:

> The bourgeois of all denominations—from the most reactionary vigilantes to the most rabid Jacobins—together with the authoritarian State communists are unanimous; that the salvation of France can and must be achieved only by and through the State. But France can be saved only by drastic measures which require the dissolution of the State . . .
> It is evident . . . that if France is to be saved, it will require spontaneous uprisings in all the provinces. Are such uprisings possible? Yes, if the workers in the great provincial cities—Lyons, Marseilles, Saint-Étienne,

Rouen and many others—have blood in their veins, brains in their heads, and if they are not doctrinaires but revolutionary socialists. Only the workers in the cities can now save France. Faced with mortal danger from within and without, France can be saved only by a spontaneous, uncompromising, passionate, anarchic and destructive uprising of the masses of the people all over France.

I believe that the only two classes now capable of so mighty an insurrection are the workers and the peasants.[12]

With revolutionary optimism Bakunin thus declared:

France as a State is finished. She can no longer save herself by regular administrative means. Now the natural France, the France of the People must enter on the scene of history, must save its own freedom and that of all Europe by an immense spontaneous and entirely popular uprising, outside all official organization, all government centralization. In sweeping from its own territories the armies of the King of Prussia, France will at the same time set free all the peoples of Europe, and accomplish the social revolution.[13]

But Bakunin was not a man who merely theorized about revolution; he was eager to participate in events, "to incarnate" principles as he put it, "into facts." On hearing of the defeats of the French armies, he became increasingly restive in Locarno. He wrote to Adolf Vogt, a friend of his last years:

My socialist revolutionary friends at Lyons are calling me to Lyons. I have made up my mind to move my old bones there and to play what will probably be my last role.[14]

He asked Vogt to give him some money so that he could travel to France. He was then fifty-six years of age. On September 9, 1870 he set out for France, arriving in Lyon six days later. At that time confusion reigned in the city. After the defeat of Sedan a republic had been immediately proclaimed in Lyons, a committee of Public Safety had been established, and several factories had been turned into national workshops. Three delegates of the committee had been sent to Paris, including Albert Richard, to negotiate with the provisional government. By the time Bakunin arrived a moderate municipal council had already been elected. Bakunin and his associates immediately created a Committee for the Salvation of France and at a public meeting on September 24, a proclamation was issued calling for the abolition of the State, the suspension of taxes and mortgages, and the establishment of a system of administration based on communes. It ended by calling on all the principle towns of France to send two delegates to a revolutionary convention in Lyons. The proclamation was posted throughout the city. A large demonstration gathered on September 28 outside the Hotel de Ville, where the municipal council usually met—although on this day most of its members had made themselves scarce. The committee took over the council chamber for a while, but the popular uprising was quickly suppressed by contingents of the National Guard. Bakunin had to go into hiding to avoid arrest, and the following day stealthily left by train to Marseilles where he spent the next three weeks at an associate's house in strict seclusion. On October 24 he left Marseilles for Locarno.

The Lyons uprising, like the Paris Commune, ended in failure and defeat. Marx seemed to side with reaction in his ridiculing of the insurrection and of Bakunin's role in it. But as Marx's biographer Franz Mehring indicated: "The ridiculing of this unsuccessful attempt might reasonably have been left to the reaction," and an opponent of Bakunin whose opposition to anarchism did not rob him of all capacity to form an objective judgement wrote:

> Unfortunately, mocking voices have been raised even in the social democratic press, although Bakunin's attempts certainly does not deserve this. Naturally, those who do not share the anarchist opinions of Bakunin and his attitude towards his baseless hopes, but apart from that, his action in Lyons was a courageous attempt to awaken the sleeping energies of the French proletariat and to direct them simultaneously against the foreign enemy and the capitalist system. Later, the Paris Commune attempted something of the sort also and was warmly praised by Marx.[15]

Bakunin spent the winter of 1870-71 in seclusion in Locarno, battling against poverty and depression. The cause of France he felt had been lost, "betrayed to the Prussians by the incapacity, the cowardice and the cupidity of the bourgeoisie." An Alliance had been formed between bureaucracy and militarism—linked to the Knout (whip) of Rus-

sian imperialism. "Goodbye to all our dreams of approaching liberation" he concluded in a letter to a friend. But in the spring of 1871
Bakunin began to feel cheerful. His friend Gambuzzi gave him a "loan"
of a thousand francs to help in the support of Antonia and the two
children, and around the same time his wife's family began to send her
a monthly allowance of fifty rubles. His economic circumstances began
to improve. He also began work on the writing of an analysis of the current political situation in Europe. As a pamphlet, the first part of "The
Knouto-Germanic Empire and the Social Revolution" was published in
July 1871. It expresses a more optimistic note, Bakunin suggesting that
even in Germany under Bismarck the workers were becoming more
and more revolutionary. He complimented the stand of the German
Socialist Workers Party who, under Bebel and Liebknecht, had resisted
the pro-war stand of the German bourgeoisie. In the same spring,
Bakunin also wrote the unfinished second part of "The Knouto-Germanic Empire and the Social Revolution," which remained un-
published during his lifetime. An extract from the manuscript was
published by two of his intimate associates, Elisée Reclus and Carlo
Cafiero, as "Dieu et L'État" (God and the State) in 1882, which was to
prove one of the most popular writings by Bakunin, and has been
republished many times in many languages.

In March 1871, Bakunin's pessimism was further alleviated by the
insurrection of the Paris Commune. When Thiers, the new head of the
French assembly—a highly reactionary body—withdrew all government officials to Versailles, it left Paris in a kind of void, with no army
and no authority of any kind apart from the central committee of the
National Guard. This was a volunteer force with radical sympathies
who were in close touch with the trade unions and the Paris Sections of
the International. Thus, the committee instituted a popular assembly
based on the universal manhood suffrage: it was to be called the "Commune of Paris." The commune was not directly inspired by Marx; in
fact most of the communards were anti-Marxists. The most important
members of the commune were Jacobins or followers of Blanqui and
Proudhon, although several anarchists were also members of the commune: Elisée Reclus, the geographer, who was director of the
Communes's library, Eugène Varlin, a close associate of Bakunin and a
leading figure in the Paris Section of the International, and Louise
Michel, the "Red Virgin," who like Reclus was to be a leading figure in
the anarchist movement towards the end of the nineteenth century.

The commune was short-lived, lasting only two months. It was
primarily concerned with its own survival and with military matters,

and its politics were reformist rather than revolutionary—only seventeen of its ninety-two members were members of the International and many of these were Proudhonists. Plans were made for secular education, night-work in bakeries was abolished, wage reductions were curtailed and factories and workshops abandoned by their owners were re-organized as co-operatives. But, as G. D. H. Cole remarked, the commune had little to show in the way of socialist reconstruction; inevitable in the circumstances for the composition of the commune's membership was largely of petit bourgeoisie origin and diverse in character.

The Paris insurrection was largely a spontaneous affair and the International was not involved in its inception at all. For two months its General Council in London remained absolutely silent as to its existence. In May, the commune was brutally suppressed, after a week of street-fighting. The exact number of casualties is not known, but around twenty thousand communards were killed in a wave of bloodshed. The brutality of the French bourgeoisie under Thiers has been ascribed to their sense of fear. Cole writes:

> The French upper classes, humiliated by the Prussians, were in double terror of revolutionary Paris; and their fears destroyed all understanding and sense of compassion. They became sheer savages, a thirst for blood. On their behalf, Thiers and his generals carried fire and sword through the street of Paris, killing and mutilating their prisoners as they advanced.[16]

Such atrocities made the Paris commune an undying memory among socialists throughout Europe. But its suppression also spelled, Cole argues, not only the end of revolutionary socialism in France—which thereafter "settled down" to the reactionary regime of the Third Republic—but also helped to destroy the International itself, for up to 1870, France had been the real centre of the International as a mass worker's party.

Three days after the collapse of the Paris Commune, Marx presented his famous address to the General Council of the International. It is subtitled "The Civil War in France." In it Marx defended the commune, seeing its measures and structure as "the glorious harbinger of a new society." It indicated a new tendency—"a government of the people by the people." He contrasted the class-based power of the modern bourgeois State—the labour—with the kind of "social republic" that the commune exemplified. The commune, he wrote, was "formed of the municipal councillors, chosen by universal suffrage in the various wards of the town, responsible and revocable at short terms. The majority of its members were naturally working men, or acknowledged representatives of the working class. The commune was to be a working, not a parliamentary, body, executive and legislative at the same time. The communal regime once established in Paris . . . the old centralized government would in the provinces, too, have given way to the self-government of the producers."[17]

The social enslavement and class despotism characteristic of the existing States was to be replaced by a "workers' State"—the dictatorship of the proletariat—and this, Marx argued, the Paris Commune heralded. The commune was not a utopian venture, not a throw-back to the medieval period; it was the setting free of elements of a new society "with which the old collapsing bourgeois society itself is pregnant."[18] The commune thus heralded the "historic mission" of the working class, the establishment of the "people's own government." This address was the closest Marx ever came to formulating a libertarian perspective. It indicates that politically Marx was a radical democrat and an advocate of universal suffrage. But Marx's homage to the Paris Commune has been seen as essentially a tactical move, for it was largely dominated by his political adversaries in France, the Blanquists and Proudhonists, and its anti-authoritarian principles were in fact in contradiction to Marx's own views of the State. As James Guillaume indicated, in the pamphlet "The Civil War in France," "Marx seems to have abandoned his own programme and gone over to the side of the federalists. Was this sincere conversion on the part of the author of *Das Kapital,* or a temporary manoeuvre dictated by events— an apparent adhesion to the commune to benefit from the prestige attached to its name?" Arthur Lehning also notes that it is an irony of history that Marx should endorse the Paris Commune, for its anti-authoritarian programmes "had nothing in common with the State socialism of Marx and was more in accord with the ideas of Proudhon and the federalist theories of Bakunin."[19]

But the Paris Commune was seen as a "working model" not only for Marx but also for the Blanquists, for whom it exemplified the revolutionary elite in action. They were critical of the Internationalists for insisting on democratic principles that they saw as inappropriate during a period of revolutionary transition. They saw democracy and socialism as something to be achieved only after the revolutionary dictatorship had destroyed the old order; not as an instrument to be employed in destroying it. Like Marx, the Blanquists advocated the necessity of taking over or establishing State power during the revolution and thus the Marxists and the Blanquists were united in their opposition to the anarchists, with both the Proudhonists and the "collectivist" anarchists headed during the Commune by Eugène Varlin. Marx differed from the Blanquists in advocating the mass organization of the proletariat as a necessary basis for the revolution, while the Blanquists remained essentially "Jacobin communists."[20] Auguste Blanqui himself did not participate in the Paris insurrection. Aged sixty-six, ill and with a price on his head, he was away from Paris. He was imprisoned immediately after the collapse of the commune where he spent most of his adult life. David Thomson's suggestion that Blanqui was the direct heir of Babeuf is valid; that he was an anarchist entirely mistaken.[21]

But G. D. H. Cole stressed that the anarchist and the anarcho-syndicalists saw the Paris commune in a very different light from that of Marx and the Blanquists.

> In their view its essence was a localism, its revolt against centralized authority, its destruction of the political State as a centre of authoritarian control. For them it was the Paris Commune, the direct expression of the right of the people of Paris to govern themselves and the model for a world-wide system of free local communes which would rid the earth of the pests of authoritarian government and centralized power. The Paris Commune was, in their view, not a State but the negation of the State.[22]

This was Bakunin's view of the 1871 commune. He expressed it in a preamble to the second part of "The Knouto-Germanic Empire and the Social Revolution" written in July 1871—two months after the commune—and published by his friend Elisée Reclus as "The Paris Commune and the Idea of the State" in Geneva in 1878. In this posthumous paper, Bakunin makes a radical distinction between two kinds of socialism. Although they agree on the fundamental aims of socialism, the authoritarian communist, on the one hand, supports the absolute power of the State, believing it necessary for the workers to seize the political power of the State, while the collectivists or revolutionary socialists, on the other hand, advocate the dissolution of the State. "The communists advocate the principle and the practices of authority; the revolutionary socialists put all their faith in liberty." And Bakunin goes on to suggest that "revolutionary socialism has just attempted its first striking and practical demonstration in the Paris Commune." He writes:

> I am a supporter of the Paris Commune, which, for all the bloodletting it suffered at the hands of the monarchical and clerical reaction, has nonetheless grown more enduring and more powerful in the hearts and minds of Europe's proletariat. I am its supporter, above all, because it was a bold, clearly formulated negation of the State.[23]

Bakunin recognized that the majority of members of the commune were not socialists, but Jacobins. Nevertheless, propelled by the instincts and aspirations of the people, which were to a high degree socialist, such Jacobins as Louis Delescluze, a veteran of the 1848 Revolution, allowed "themselves to be carried along into a social revolution."[24] Bakunin thus concluded:

> Contrary to the belief of authoritarian communists— which I deem completely wrong—that a social revolution must be decreed and organized either by a dictatorship or a constituent assembly emerging from a political revolution, our friends, the Paris socialists, believed that revolution could neither be made nor brought to its full development except by the spontaneous and continued action of the masses, the groups and associations of the people.[25]

Bakunin goes on to offer a critique of the State, and religious metaphysics.

Indirectly, Bakunin's defence of the Paris Commune, which broke out on the eve of Bakunin's visit to Florence, led to a considerable increase in his influence in Italy, for the veteran revolutionary nationalist Giuseppe Mazzini had added his voice to those of the reactionary critics who cursed the commune and the International. In July 1871, Mazzini warned Italian workers about the International, seeing it as a materialist and anti-religious movement. Around the same time, this "saintly old man," as Bakunin described him, harshly denounced the commune as being anti-nationalist, anti-religious and immoral. Bakunin and Mazzini had long known each other and Bakunin seems to have had a lot of love and respect for the famous Italian patriot

"whose incomparable purity shines out so brightly amid the corruption
of the century." But Mazzini's attacks on the commune and the International aroused Bakunin's fury and, in August 1871, he published a
"Response of an Internationalist to Mazzini," which appeared in both
French and Italian. This work, Guillaume suggests, made a deep impression on Italian working people, producing a climate of opinion
which spawned, towards the end of 1871, many new sections of the International. The work is a defence of the materialist and atheistic outlook and is highly critical of Mazzini's political idealism and
theological standpoint. Who now stands under the barrier of God?,
Bakunin asks: Napoleon III and Bismarck, all the emperors, kings and
privileged elite of Europe, all the blood-suckers of industry, commerce
and banking; all the teachers and savants of the State—priests, gen-
darmes, jailers and police. This is the barrier under which Mazzini now
stands. And Bakunin continues:

> Where were the materialists and atheists yesterday, for all
> to see? In the Paris Commune. And what about the
> idealists, the believers in God? In the National Assembly
> at Versailles. What did the men of Paris want? The final
> emancipation of labour. And what does the triumphant
> Assembly of Versailles seek now? Its final degradation
> under the double yoke of the spiritual and temporal
> power...
> At the very moment when the heroic populace of
> Paris, in its noblest hour, was being massacred in its tens of
> thousands, women and children and all, in defence of the
> most humane, the most just and highest cause that history
> had ever seen, the cause of the emancipation of workers
> all over the world; at the moment when the hideous coali-
> tion of all the obscene reactionaries who today are
> celebrating their victorious blood-bath at Versailles, not
> content with the mass-murder and imprisonment of our
> brothers and sisters of the Paris Commune... Mazzini, the
> great Mazzini, the pure democraty, turns his back on the
> cause of the proletariat, forgets everything but his mission
> as a priest or prophet, and weighs in with his own out-
> rages also! He has the audacity to deny not only the justice
> of their cause but also their sublime, heroic dedication
> and portrays the people who gave up their lives for the
> deliverance of all the world as a common mob, ignorant of

all moral law and obeying only savage, self-seeking urges.[26]

A second pamphlet entitled "The Political Theology of Mazzini and the International" was published by Guillaume at the end of 1871, and this further consolidated and extended the International in Italy. In November 1871, a workers' congress was organized by the followers of Mazzini and held in Rome. Bakunin wrote a "Circular to my Italian Friends," which was printed and distributed to the delegates. This led to three delegates at the congress, including Carlo Cafiero, to vote against the proposals of Mazzini, whose principles they considered "contrary to the best interest of the working class and to the cause of humanity."[27] Thus, a division emerged within the Italian workers' movement between the followers of Mazzini and Bakunin, but as Garibaldi came to support the International, Bakunin's socialist supporters soon gained ascendancy. For Mazzini's movement, though revolutionary in its beginnings, was almost exclusively a nationalist movement and its leadership was largely in the hands of middle-class professionals. Mazzini, who died in March 1872, had a deep hatred of class-conflict, regarding this as undermining the national unity. Dissidents within Mazzini's movement held a congress in Bologna in December 1871 and formed a new body—*Il Fascio Operaio*—to promote united action by the left wing of the workers; a movement against the Mazzinists. "*Fascio*"—the bundle of staves tied together, giving strength without full unification—stood, not for what is now known as fascism, but, as Cole writes, for the federal unity of the local workers' groups. The groups of *Fascio* were essentially anarchist, and in full sympathy with Bakunin and the Swiss opponents of the IWMA General Council.[28]

Bakunin was also instrumental in the creation of the International in Spain, for it was the Italian, Giuseppe Fanelli, at Bakunin's behest, who was mainly responsible for founding the first branches of the International in Madrid and Barcelona in the autumn of 1868. Fanelli had worked with Bakunin in the League of Peace and Freedom and seceded with him from the League to the International. In Madrid, Fanelli came into sharp conflict with Marx's son-in-law Paul Lafargue who started a rival Madrid section that was supported by the General Council in London. Although Bakunin took no direct part in the Spanish movement, the International in Spain largely followed Bakunin's own brand of revolutionary socialism and was essentially anarchist in outlook. The two Spanish delegates to the Basel congress in 1809, Gaspar Sentinon and Rafael Farga-Pellicer, were both followers of Bakunin, having enrolled in the Geneva section of the Alliance. Bakunin kept up a lively correspondence with both men throughout 1870 and 1871. Anselmo Lorenzo, who came to represent Spain at the London conference of the International in 1871, was also a supporter of Bakunin as well as the author of numerous books expounding the doctrines of collectivist anarchism.

NOTES

1.   Carr, E. H. 1937. *Michael Bakunin,* New York: Knopf, p. 384.
2.   Lampert, E. 1957. *Studies in Religion,* London: Routledge & Kegan Paul, p. 144.
3.   Ulam, A. 1965. *Lenin and the Bolsheviks.* London: Collins/Fontana, p. 54.
4.   Carr, op. cit., p. 385.
5.   Nomad, M. 1933. *Apostles of Revolution.* New York: Collier, pp. 230-35.
6.   Carr, op. cit., p. 395.
7.   Masters, A. 1974. *Bakunin: The Father of Anarchism,* London: Sidgwick and Jackson, p. 187.
8.   Carr, op. cit., p. 406.
9.   Masters, op. cit., p. 203.
10. Guillaume in Dolgoff, S., ed., trans., introd., 1973. *Bakunin on Anarchy,* New York: Knopf, p. 40.
11. For useful studies of Nechaev see Nomad, M. 1933. *Apostles of Revolution.* New York: Collier, p. 214-256 and Avrich, P. 1974, *Bakunin and Nechaev,* London: Freedom Press.
12. Dolgoff, op. cit., pp. 187-89.
13. Woodcock, p. 163.
14. Carr, op. cit., p. 411.
15. Mehring, F. 1936. *Karl Marx: His Life and Thought,* London: Macmillian. 1936: 467 quoted in Masters 1974: 223.
16. Cole, G.D.H., 1954. *Marxism and Anarchism 1850-1890, History of Socialist Thought, Vol. II, Marxism and Anarchism 1850-1890.* London: Macmillan, p. 161.
17. Marx, K. & Engels, F. 1968. *Selected Works,* London: Lawrence & Wishort, pp. 287-88.
18. McLelland, D. 1973. *Karl Marx: His Life and Thought.* London: Macmillan, p. 398.
19. Dolgoff, op. cit., pp. 259-60.
20. Cole, op. cit., pp. 166-67.
21. Thomson, D. 1964. *Democracy in France Since 1870.* Oxford University Press, p. 25.
22. Cole, op. cit., p. 167.
23. Dolgoff, op. cit., pp. 262-64.
24. Dolgoff, op. cit., p. 267.
25. Dolgoff, op. cit., p. 268.
26. Lehning, A. 1973. *Michael Bakunin: Selected Writings.* London: Cape, pp. 220-23.
27. Carr, op. cit., p. 435.
28. Cole, op. cit., p. 183.

Chapter 6

Decline and Fall of the First International

BETWEEN the Basel congress of the International in 1869 and the end of 1871 there had been a great growth of the International in both Italy and Spain—largely due to the influence of Bakunin. In 1870, at a general congress in Barcelona one hundred and fifty societies from thirty-six regions constituted the Spanish Regional Federation and adopted as their status those of the Jura Federation. This had been drawn-up by Bakunin. Thus, while the International was experiencing a marked decline in membership and considerable apathy in the industrial countries, particularly in Britain where Marx was residing, in the Latin countries the International was expanding by leaps and bounds. And wherever it was spreading it was doing so, as Paul Thomas writes, "under the mantle of Bakuninism."[1] Thomas even hints that Marx's "The Civil War in France" was a calculated move, using the symbolism of the Paris Commune to reunify a disparate movement. But there was little awareness at that time among most adherents of the International of the doctrinal differences separating Bakunin from Marx—except in Switzerland. And, it was in Switzerland that the latent schism between two very different concepts of socialism—Marxism and collectivist anarchism—first began to be articulated in institutional terms.

At the end of 1869, Nicholas Utin arrived in Geneva and in January 1870, as Bakunin was leaving for Locarno, Utin established himself as an editor of *L'Égalité*. Utin had an intense dislike for Bakunin and soon took every opportunity to denounce him as an advocate of pan-Slavism—though Bakunin had long since abandoned his nationalist tendencies. A Russian exile like Bakunin, Utin also began to spread the old rumour that Bakunin was a Tsarist agent. Later that same month, January 1870, Utin organized a Russian section of the International in Geneva—in direct opposition to Bakunin's Alliance—and applied to the General Council in London for recognition. He also asked Marx, whom he addressed as the "Venerable Dr. Marx," to become the representative for Russia on the General Council. Marx found this all rather strange but seems to have accepted the proposal especially as Utin also mentioned that it would be among one of the tasks of the new section to publicly "unmask Bakunin." Thereafter, Utin continued to supply Marx with a steady flow of information, or misinformation, about Bakunin, and played a considerable part in poisoning the relations between the two men, although Marx had long harboured quite unfounded suspicions that Bakunin was simply a political intriguer who was out to "wreck" the International. If anything, Bakunin did far more to expand the membership of the International than did Marx himself, who had little influence on the English trade unionists. Significantly, after having helped to destroy the International, Utin made his peace with Czardom, returned to Russia and ended his days as a wealthy and respectable government contractor.[2]

In April 1870, the annual congress of the Federation Romande, consisting of sections of the International in French-speaking Switzerland, was held in the little town of La Chaux-de-Fonds in the Jura. Utin took the opportunity, in Bakunin's absence, to launch a bitter personal attack on Bakunin quoting from Nechaev's "Revolutionary Catechism" to imply that Bakunin in his revolutionary activities recognized neither justice nor morality and was essentially a nihilist. This all arose in the debate regarding the application of the Geneva section of the Alliance for admission to the Federation. Guillaume spoke in defence of Bakunin, and the Alliance was eventually admitted into the Federation by a majority vote. This led to a virtual split in the International in Switzerland with the Geneva sections under the leadership of Utin following Marx and the General Council, while the Jura sections became fervent supporters of Bakunin. James Guillaume and Adhemar Schwitzguebel were leading members of the latter group, which became known as the Jura Federation. The General Council in London eventually agreed to accept both the Geneva Federation and the Jura Federation as affiliated bodies of the International. It is important to stress that this split represents a genuine disagreement within the International between the libertarian and State socialists. G. D. H. Cole expressed this cogently. He wrote:

> This conflict of views was not the outcome of any "conspiracy" either on Bakunin's part or on that of Marx. It arose out of real differences both in attitude and in the character of the movements of which the International was made up. Bakunin and Guillaume, and the Spanish and Italian leaders, did carry on an increasingly active propaganda against Marx and the General Council; but there was nothing particularly conspiratorial about it,

unless one counts Bakunin's habitual tendency to give
his most commonplace activities a conspiratorial tone.
Marx, for his part, intensely irritated by what he
regarded as the unrealistic folly of the anarchists, had
developed an aggravated form of conspiracy-mania,
which led him to see the entire anti-authoritarian movement as a sinister conspiracy directed against himself.[3]

The conflict between Marx and Bakunin, however, came to a head
in the sham conference of the International held in London in September 1871. Given the widespread support for Bakunin and his anarchism
among Internationalists in Spain, Belgium, Italy and the Jura section of
Switzerland, it was clear that Marx and the General Council could only
defeat Bakunin by "upstaging" him.[4] The London conference was
therefore a largely private and secret affair. It consisted only of the
General Council and invited guests—almost entirely partisans of Marx.
Two delegates were invited from Switzerland—one of whom was Utin.
The Jura Federation was not invited, and Spain had only one representative and Italy none. Because of the war, Germany had no
delegates, and France was represented only by refugees—mostly Blanquists. The dice, as E. H. Carr put it, had been well and truly loaded
against Bakunin. Besides implying that anarchism was almost a heresy
and forbidding the formation of separate sections, one of the most important decisions taken by the London conference was to declare the
necessity for workers in each country to form their own political party,
independent of the bourgeois parties. With the complete absence of the
anarchists, and with the support of the Blanquists, such a resolution
was easily carried.

The Swiss groups of the International, all Bakuninists and hostile
to Marx, immediately organized their own conference at Sonvillier in
the Jura in November 1871. Bakunin could not attend, and the leading
spirits of the meeting were Guillaume, Spichiger and Schwitzguebel.
They immediately repudiated any of the London decisions, refusing to
recognize that the London conference was a properly constituted
organ of the International. They denounced the autocratic powers exercised by the General Council, and called for the reaffirmation of an
International that was composed of a free federation of autonomous
sections instead of one governed by a General Council. The congress
produced the "Sonvillier Circular," which demanded an immediate
congress of the International to debate its structure. The circular was
sympathetically received not only in Spain and Italy, but also in Bel-

gium. As a result, the General Council was obliged to announce a congress at The Hague in September 1872. It was clear that this meeting would prove to be an important encounter between the Marxist and the anarchist (i.e. Bakuninist) sections of the International. As it turned out, it proved to be the last real meeting of the First International.

The Sonvillier Circular was a critique of the basic doctrine formulated by the General Council of the International, namely the importance of "the conquest of political power by the working class." The circular counterposed this doctrine with the notion that a social revolution should involve the "emancipation of the workers by the workers themselves" and that:

> The future society must be nothing else than the universalization of the organization that the International has formed for itself. We must therefore strive to make this organization as close as possible to our ideal. How could one expect an egalitarian society to emerge out of an authoritarian organization? It is impossible. The International, embryo of the future society, must from now on faithfully reflect our principles of federation and liberty, and must reject any principle tending toward authority and dictatorship.[5]

Bakunin enthusiastically welcomed the Sonvillier Circular and devoted his energies to actively propagating its principles. Marx responded to it by issuing, as a circular from the General Council, a pamphlet entitled "Fictitious Splits in the International." It was printed in Geneva and sent to all sections of the International. It outlined Marx's own views on Bakunin, and his opinion of the events surrounding the formation of the International Alliance of Socialist Democracy. Marx was critical of Bakunin on a number of grounds: his advocacy of total abstention from politics; his attempt to create an "international within the International" thereby creating confusion between the programme of the International Working Men's Association (identified with Marx's own ideas) and Bakunin's makeshift programme; his assertion that making the International an embryonic egalitarian society would only weaken the organization in its fight against the exploiters. Marx seems to have seen Bakunin's Alliance as a kind of sectarian organization like those of the early utopian socialists, which could only inhibit the formation of the International as "a militant organization of the proletarian class of all countries." He also saw the various radical manifestos by Bakunin as "verbiage" which would be useful in promoting the aims of the reactionaries, the implication being that one shouldn't publish radical manifestos in case they upset or helped the bourgeoisie. Yet Marx's pamphlet indicates an underlying ambivalence, for he wants to believe that the splits in the International are all of a "fictitious" nature and that the Bakuninist groups are "sham sections" that have either no reality or are small cliques composed not of real workers but of lawyers, journalists and other "bourgeois doctrinaires." This coming from a man who studied law at university, earned a living as a journalist (as well as being supported by Engels) and whose whole lifestyle was thoroughly bourgeois. Marx was also obsessed with the idea that Bakunin was an intriguer who intended to replace the General Council with his own personal dictatorship. Guillaume and other supporters of Bakunin found Marx's pamphlet full of personal slander. Bakunin is said to have described it as a "heap of filth."

The all-important congress at The Hague was duly held in early September 1872. Sixty-four delegates attended the congress, the majority of whom were supporters of Marx, for the Italians had decided to boycott the meeting. In August 1872, the first national congress of Italian Socialism was held in Rimini and there formed an Italian Federation of the International. The congress denounced the "slander and mystification" of the General Council, and Marx's "lust for authority" and therefore resolved to break all solidarity with the General Council. It proposed "to all those sections who do not share the authoritarian principles of the General Council to send their representatives on September 2nd 1872 not to The Hague but to Neuchatel in Switzerland for the purpose of opening ... (an) anti-authoritarian congress."[6] Bakunin, who could not attend the congress, lost much of his support at the congress, and only six delegates, two from the Jura and four from Spain were supporters of Bakunin. The General Council, made up largely of Marx's followers and Blanquists, and the German State socialists formed the bulk of Marx's support. Again Marx had engineered a congress that was packed with his own supporters. But it was clear that Marx aimed to defeat Bakunin—and the ideas he propagated—not only by weight of numbers, but also by destroying his personal reputation. To this end, Engels drafted a long report at the request of the General Council aiming to demonstrate that Bakunin had founded a secret society, the Alliance (the main organ of which was the Central Committee of the Jura Federation), whose aims were incompatible with those of the International which it sought, it said, to disorganize and dominate. Engels therefore proposed that the congress should expel Bakunin and all present members of the Alliance of Socialist Democracy (including the Jura Federation) from the International Working Men's Association. On the last day of the congress—after one third of the delegates had already gone home—this proposal was put before congress and by a vote of twenty-seven for and seven against—with eight abstentions—Bakunin (along with his friend Guillaume) was expelled from the International.

Although there was little evidence that the Alliance had existed as a secret society after 1869, Bakunin was nevertheless condemned. What seemed to have swayed the committee of inquiry that had been set up to examine the allegations was that Marx produced—behind closed doors—a copy of the letter that Nechaev had written to Bakunin's publishers regarding the translation of Marx's *Das Kapital*. Bakunin was therefore unfairly dismissed from the International on two grounds:

1. That he had tried to establish and perhaps succeeded in establishing a society in Europe named "The Alliance" with rules, social and political matters entirely different from those of the International.

2. That Bakunin had made use of deceptive tricks in order to appropriate some portion of another person's fortune, which constitutes fraud.[7]

It was clear that Marx was determined to remove Bakunin from the International even if he had to use the most underhand methods to do it.

But the bombshell at the 1872 congress was the startling proposal, presented by Marx and the General Council, that the seat of the General Council of the International should be transferred to New York. It came as a complete surprise to most of the assembled delegates, although they voted for the proposal nonetheless. What Marx's motives were for such a move has been debated, but in doing this, he effectively killed off the International. But at least, by removing it to New York, he had saved the International from the influence of Bakunin.

Immediately after The Hague congress, the anarchist members of the International held their own congress, convening at St. Imier in Switzerland. It comprised delegations from Spain, Italy and the Swiss Jura. It was a small gathering, and the delegates unanimously rejected the decisions of The Hague congress and the powers given to the new General Council. They constituted themselves into a free union of federation of the International, bound together not by an autocratic council, but by solidarity and mutual friendship. For a while, two rival internationals continued to exist, but by the end of the decade the First International Working Men's Association had essentially ceased to function. The International congress held in Geneva in September 1873 was perhaps the last viable meeting. The congress dissolved with the General Council and declared the International a free federation of autonomous sections each with a right to reorganize itself as it saw fit.

NOTES

1.   Thomas, P. 1980. *Karl Marx and the Anarchists*. London: Routledge & Kegan Paul,
     p. 319.
2.   Cole, G.D.H., 1954. *History of Socialist Thought, Vol. II, Marxism and Anarchism
     1850-1890*. London: Macmillan, p. 197.
3.   Cole, op. cit., p. 193.
4.   Thomas, op. cit., p. 320.
5.   Guillaume in Dolgoff, S., ed., trans., introd., 1973. *Bakunin on Anarchy*, New
     York: Knopf, p. 45.
6.   Hostetter, R. 1958. *The Italian Socialist Movement*. Princeton, NJ: Van Nostrand,
     p. 284.
7.   Guillaume in Dolgoff, op. cit., p. 47.

Chapter 7

Last Years

I N June 1872, on hearing of the death of her only surviving brother, Bakunin's wife Antonia decided to return to Russia with her children, in order to care for her aging parents. She was to remain in Russia for two years. Deprived of his family and feeling lonely, Bakunin moved from Locarno and settled in Zurich, then a haven of political refugees from Russia. He was soon surrounded by a group of devotees and became actively engaged in political activities. One of the most important of his acquaintances was an energetic young man named Michael Sazhin, better known by his pseudonym Armand Ross. Together with Bakunin and other young friends, Ross formed a small anarchist group, for which Bakunin drafted a constitution. Bakunin also became involved in a dispute with another Russian emigré, Peter Lavrov, who had also settled in Zurich. After this sojourn in Zurich, Bakunin spent from October 1872 to September 1874 again in Locarno—quietly working at intervals on the second part of his *Knouto-Germanic Empire* and corresponding at length with his anarchist colleagues in Italy and Spain—where he now had a large following. In September 1872, his tranquillity was shattered by the publication of the pamphlet "The Alliance of the Socialist Democracy and the International Working Men's Association." Published anonymously in London, and in French, it appears to have been written mainly by Engels and Marx's son-in-law Paul Lafargue. The pamphlet is a defence of the General Council's decision to expel Bakunin from the International, and derides Bakunin's involvement in the Lyons insurrection, portraying him as solely a revolutionary who advocates secret societies, brigandage, political assassinations and pan-destruction. Quoting from one of Nechaev's pamphlets, it virtually equates Bakunin's anarchism with Nechaev's nihilism. "They want to annihilate and amorphise everything, absolutely everything. They draw up lists of proscribed persons, doomed to die by their daggers, their position, their ropes, by bullets from their revolvers . . . but they will bow before the majesty of the Tsar."[1]

The pamphlet is a slanderous misrepresentation of Bakunin's essential thoughts. He was accused of being the "Pope" of a "modern society of Jesus" (i.e. Jesuit) committed to fraud, crime and assassination. Nettlau rightly described it as a "scurrilous pamphlet."[2]

Quite apart from being unfairly expelled from the International, these "Marxist falsifications" hurt Bakunin deeply. He wrote a long reply to the *Journal of Geneve* (September 26) expressing his despair with Marx, whom he felt was the main instigator of the pamphlet. It showed that Marx was all too ready to assume the role of a police agent, an informer and a slanderer. The letter concluded on a weary, rather despairing note:

> Shall I confess it? All this has disgusted me profoundly with public life. I have had enough of it, and, having passed all my life in the struggle I am weary of it. I am past sixty and an affection of the heart, which grows worse with age, makes life more and more difficult for me. Let other and younger men take up the work. For myself, I feel neither the strength nor perhaps, the confidence which are required to go on rolling Sisyphus's stone against the triumphant forces of reaction . . . henceforth I shall trouble no man's repose; and I ask, in my turn, to be left in peace.[3]

The following month (October 12, 1873) he wrote a letter of resignation to the "Comrades of the Jura Federation." He was physically too weak he said to continue the struggle and in the camp of the proletariat he could only be an obstacle, not a help. He wrote:

> I will retire then, dear comrades, full of gratitude to you and sympathy for your great and holy cause, the cause of humanity. With brotherly concern I will avidly watch your progress and salute with joy each of your new triumphs. Until death I will be yours.

And he concluded:

> Organize ever more strongly the practical militant solidarity of the workers of all trades in all countries, and remember that infinitely weak as you may be as individuals, you will constitute an immense irresistible force when organized and united in the universal collectively.[4]

This hardly sounds like a nihilist bent on pan-destruction and in-surrectory assassination, anticipating an "imminent revolution" as the pamphlet written by Engels and Lafargue portrayed Bakunin.

His lifelong battles and years of imprisonment, and his dissolute style of life had clearly taken their toll on Bakunin, and by the summer of 1873 he was physically exhausted. He now craved repose and retire-ment—thoughts that were crystallized by the harsh critiques of the Marxists. He had grown to immense proportions and suffered from a heart complaint which made physical exertion difficult, as well as from asthma. In October 1873 there was something of a respite for Bakunin. His friend Carlo Cafiero had recently inherited a large sum of money and decided to put these funds to the services of the revolution. A large property was therefore bought near Locarno, a house called Baronata, situated on the road to Bellinzona, and close to the lake. The property was registered in Bakunin's name, and aimed to provide a settled house for the aging Bakunin as well as a refuge for international revo-lutionaries. Bakunin and Cafiero attempted to turn the property into a self-supporting commune, and lavishly spent thousands of francs on building a new house and on the most impractical purchases—think-ing funds from Cafiero's inheritance unlimited. Antonia returned from Russia in the spring of 1874 with her children, parents and her married sister, and Cafiero also came to live at Baronata with his new wife Olympia. Unfortunately, the whole enterprise turned into a nightmare for Cafiero discovered that his resources were not unlimited and that he had wasted his entire fortune. Relations between the two men be-came strained and Bakunin, to relieve the situation, had to sign over the property to Cafiero.

But in spite of these difficulties and his strained relations with both Cafiero and his wife Antonia—Bakunin could not resist joining the in-surrectionary movement in Bologna in July 1874. But the insurrection was poorly planned and the plot miscarried, and Bakunin was forced to return to Switzerland disguised as an infirm country priest.

After a short period of separation, having left Locarno in the sum-mer, Bakunin was eventually to reunite with his wife in September 1874. Unsure about living with him again she eventually relented and invited him to join her. "Broken, his mind wandering, sometimes filled with feverish plans and sometimes with despair, Michael gratefully returned to his much neglected wife."[5] It was, as Carr notes, a balm to his troubled spirit.

Bakunin's health was now deteriorating fast. Besides his asthma and cardiac problem, he was also suffering from incontinence, dropsy and deafness. At times he also suffered loss of memory. By the end of 1875 he was only a shadow of his former self. He also again found himself deeply in debt, and decided to move to Naples. In June 1876, Antonia left for Italy to present a petition to the Minister of the Interior, while Bakunin went to visit his old friend and medical advisor Adolf Vogt in Berne. He reached Berne on June 14 and was taken to hospital where he was affectionately attended by Dr. Vogt and his other close friends, the Reichels. Two weeks later Bakunin went into a coma, and he died at midday on July 1, 1876.

The funeral was held two days later; a group of about forty comrades and friends attended, mostly from the Jura Federation including James Guillaume, Elisée Reclus and Adhemar Schwitzguebel. Thus passed away Michael Bakunin: "contradictory, erratic, given to wild enthusiasms, insolvent, lonely, unpredictable, creatively destructive—and essentially the father of anarchism."[6]

NOTES

1. Marx, K. & Engels, F. 1968. *Selected Works*, London: Lawrence & Wishort, pp. 117-18.
2. Nettlau, M. 1976. *Writings on Bakunin*. London: C. Slienger, 15.
3. Carr, E. H. 1937. *Michael Bakunin*, New York: Knopf, p. 478.
4. Dolgoff, S. 1973. ed., trans, introd., *Bakunin on Anarchy*, New York: Knopf, p. 353.
5. Masters, A. 1974. *Bakunin: The Father of Anarchism*, London: Sidgwich and Jackson, p. 245.
6. Masters, op. cit., p. 262.

Part Two: Collectivist Anarchism

Chapter 8

Preamble

MAX NETTLAU wrote that individuals who have a creative influence on their own age belong to four descriptions; they are prophets or dreamers, thinkers or rebels. Of those who have struggled for the freedom and social well-being of humankind and have combined these four roles, perhaps the best known was Michael Bakunin. Heroic rebels have always existed but they tend to have a narrow vision. Great thinkers are found in abundance, but their "theories" and "systems" are often remote from human concerns and everyday life. Dreamers and prophets likewise are often enwrapped in their own thoughts and visions. What is unique about Bakunin as a political figure is that he combined all four creative roles—prophet, dreamer, rebel and thinker.[1] But while various scholars have only been too happy to stress the visionary and rebellious aspects of Bakunin's personality, they have too often belittled Bakunin's achievement as a political thinker. Marxists, in particular, have tended to repeat parrot-fashion the opinions of their "founder" and Bakunin is thus dismissed as a pre-Marxist "petty-bourgeois ideologue," an "ignoramus," "a Mohammed without a Koran," "a non-entity as a theoretician," the writer who could only produce a "children's primer"—to cite some of the derogatory and quite misleading epithets of Marx.

Liberal scholars have been even more vociferous in downplaying or deriding Bakunin's stature as a political thinker. The classic example of this is Isaiah Berlin's famous essay "Herzen and Bakunin on Individual Liberty." There is no doubting Berlin's scholarship and intellectual brilliance, but his portrayal of Bakunin is biased, crude and unfair. He notes the important similarities between these two important revolutionary figures of the nineteenth century. Although very different in attitude and temperament, both Bakunin and Herzen were at one in placing individual liberty at the centre of their thought and action, and both dedicated their lives to struggling against all forms of oppression—whether social or political. Both shared an acute antipathy to Marxism and saw no gain in replacing one form of despotism with another. But there the comparison ends, for Bakunin is seen by Berlin as little more than a gifted journalist, while Herzen is described as a political thinker of the first rank, on par with Marx and Tocqueville, and as a moralist more interesting and original than either. Bakunin, Berlin writes, "for all his clever, vigorous, at times devastating, critical power, seldom says anything which is precise or profound, or authentic—in any sense, personally "lived through"— while Herzen expresses bold and original ideas and is a political thinker of the first importance.[2] Berlin plays on this contrast throughout the essay and continues:

> Bakunin's thought is almost always simple, shallow and clear; the language is passionate, direct and imprecise, riding from climax to climax of rhetorical evidence, sometimes expository, more often hortatory or polemical, usually ironical, sometimes sparkling, always gay, always entertaining, always readable, seldom related to facts or experience, never original or serious or specific.[3]

Bakunin, Berlin concludes with great panache, is not a serious thinker and,

> . . . what is to be looked for in him is not social theory or political doctrine, but an outlook and a temperament. There are no coherent ideas to be extracted from his writings of any period, only fire and imagination, violence and poetry, and an ungovernable desire for strong sensations, for life at a high tension, for the disintegration of all that is peaceful, secluded, tidy, orderly, small scale, Philistine, established, moderate, part of the monotonous prose of daily life . . . Bakunin, the official friend of absolute liberty, has not bequeathed a single idea worth considering for its own sake; there is not a fresh thought, not even an authentic emotion, only annoying diatribes, high spirits, malicious vignettes and a memorable epigram or two.[4]

All these fine sounding words come from a scholar who is described as one of the most outstanding liberal intellects of this century, yet they convey little more than a travesty of Bakunin's life and work. Had Berlin bothered to seriously look for a political theory within Bakunin's writings he would easily have found one. It was the theory of "collectivist" anarchism, and Bakunin's thoughts on this theory, though by no means systematic, are both important and original. Berlin's thesis is back to front. It was Bakunin who was the original thinker, for the anarchism he propounded was then a new political doctrine, while Herzen had nothing to offer that was original in the way of a coherent theory. For in essence he was simply a radical liberal who advocated, like other liberals, the need for constitutional government—although he was a good deal more socialist than classical liberals like Mill. And Bakunin had a good deal more sense of reality, and his ideas were much more in touch with "facts" and "experiences" than those of Berlin, for he realized, as we shall see, that all the liberal claptrap about "liberty" was meaningless unless it took into account the economic realities of capitalism. It is Berlin, not Bakunin, who has an abstract concept of liberty. Certainly Bakunin hated order, seclusion, the quiet life—something that must be quite upsetting to an Oxford scholar!

But Berlin's essay is further disfigured by his unwarranted suggestion—using Bakunin's friend Herzen as his authority—that Bakunin was, like Robespierre, an advocate of violence against people and an enemy of real liberty. Bakunin, he implies, had a "cynical indifference to the fate of individual human beings" and had a "childish enthusiasm" for playing with human lives for the sake of social experiment. Berlin acknowledges that Bakunin dedicated his entire life to the struggle for liberty:

> He fought for it in action and in words. More than any other individual in Europe he stood for ceaseless rebellion against every form of constitutional authority, for ceaseless protest in the name of the insulted and oppressed of every nation and class.[5]

Yet, Berlin cannot avoid insinuating that Bakunin loved humanity only in the abstract and "was prepared, like Robespierre, to wade through seas of blood," and thus was akin to Attila and had a "fascist streak." Such a conclusion is an insult to Bakunin, and a blot on Berlin's liberal scholarship.

The downplaying of Bakunin's intellectual stature, and a refusal to accept him as a serious political thinker in his own right, is widely accepted in the literature. While Proudhon, Stirner, Kropotkin and, of course, Marx, have all been the subject of numerous intellectual appraisals, apart from the study by Eugene Pyziur (1955) and some short articles, Bakunin's anarchism has not been discussed anywhere with the seriousness it deserves. Additionally, almost all biographers of Bakunin are interested only in his life and personality—particularly in trying to unravel the complexities of his psyche—and treat his ideas as either unimportant or so perverse as not to be taken seriously. E. H. Carr, for example, devoted only seven pages of his biography—which runs to over five hundred pages—to a discussion of Bakunin's anarchism. His portrayal of Bakunin as an advocate of "extreme individualism," as in essence a Hegelian idealist, and as a precursor of Italian fascism[6], only indicates his own theoretical naivety and a failure to understand what Bakunin's anarchism entailed.

Bakunin, as all writers have acknowledged, friends and foes alike, was not a systematic thinker. As Carr writes:

> Few men whose life and thought have exercised so powerful an influence on the world as those of Michael Bakunin have left so confused and imperfect a record of their opinions.[7]

He was too much involved in revolutionary activity to have the time, like Marx, to sit around in the library of some great museum, to study and write systematic works. Much of his influence was the result of his letter-writing—and he was a prodigious letter-writer, sometimes composing twenty or more letters in a day, and such letters often had the proportions of a pamphlet. His literary output was in fact enormous, and yet he did not leave a single finished book to prosperity. Almost all his writings are part of his revolutionary activity, and thus are fragmentary and have a polemical or expository quality. He was both a prolific and a lucid writer, who knew, as Rocker wrote, "how to put ardour and enthusiasm and fire into his words." Landauer in fact remarked that few dissertations were written as vividly as Bakunin's works.[8] Although not quite as lyrical as Berlin makes out—Bakunin was certainly no Herzen or Nietzsche—Bakunin's writings have a transparency, eloquence, warmth and readability that is matched by few other political thinkers.

But the important point is that Bakunin made no effort to be systematic and was critical of the implications of grand theories that purported to explain the human condition in terms of abstract concepts. The efforts of liberal scholars like Berlin and Kelly to foist upon Bakunin an obsessive attachment to the abstract concepts of Hegelian idealism seems to me to indicate a woeful misunderstanding of Bakunin's whole approach to life—as well as a certain naivety in their understanding of Hegel's own project. Paul Avrich, I think, is closer to the substance of Bakunin's thought when he writes:

> He refused to recognize any preordained laws of history. He rejected the view that social change depends on the gradual unfolding of "objective" historical conditions. He believed, on the contrary, that individuals shape their own destinies, that their lives cannot be squeezed into a Procrustean bed of abstract sociological formulas.[9]

Bakunin explicitly contrasted his own approach to that of Marx. He considered himself neither a scholar, nor philosopher, nor even a writer by vocation and wrote to an anarchist colleague in Spain, Anselmo Lorenzo:

> You know, citizen, that whenever it pleases them, they (Marx's followers) depict me as the head of a school of the "International" which they call anarchist. This is an honour and dishonour which I do not deserve under any circumstance. I am not a philosopher, and not a creator of systems like Marx.[10]

To another associate he wrote:

> No theory, no ready-made system, no book that has ever been written will save the world. I cleave to no system. I am a true seeker.[11]

But it is misleading I think to infer from this that Bakunin was a theoretical nihilist, or a proponent of a romantic strain of "anti-intellectualism." Like other anarchists, Bakunin certainly harboured a deep-seated distrust of rational systems and of the intellectuals who constructed them but, as we shall see, Bakunin's criticisms were aimed at idealist systems and the rule of an intelligentsia rather than against the rational use of the intellect. For, like his mentors Hegel and Marx, Bakunin stressed the importance of reason, the "power to think," considering this one of the most precious of the human faculties.

It is my contention that although Bakunin's writings are indeed unsystematic and fragmentary, they convey, as Maximoff (1953) has tried to indicate in an important anthology of his writings, a consistent and fairly systematic political theory, which Bakunin himself described as revolutionary socialism or collectivist anarchism. Bakunin's formulation of this doctrine in the last decade of his life signals Bakunin out as a highly original political thinker, certainly one on par with Hobbes, Rousseau and Marx.

Many of Bakunin's ideas were, of course, not original, but then what scholar does not draw upon and develop the ideas of his or her predecessors? The genealogy of Bakunin's thought can be traced, as Pyziur suggests,[12] primarily to four intellectual sources: Hegel, Feuerbach, Proudhon and Marx, but what is important about Bakunin is that he uses these ideas to form a new creative synthesis—collectivist anarchism. The anarcho-communism, or communist anarchism formulated in the decades between 1870 and 1920 by such theorists as Cafiero, Reclus, Kropotkin and Berkman, was in essence a development and elaboration of the key ideas that Bakunin had expressed at the end of his life. When Engels wrote to Cafiero (July 1, 1871) that "Bakunin has a theory of his own, consisting more or less of a mixture of communism and Proudhonism," though meant as an insult, he was expressing an essential truth.[13] And when a contemporary writer suggests that the anarchist "is forever torn between the liberal values of individuality, independence, autonomy, privacy and self-determination, on the one hand, and the non-liberal values of community, solidarity and the encouragement of virtue through social pressure on the other,"[14] he precisely forgets that anarchism, as formulated by Bakunin, is a political philosophy that insists on the necessary integration of liberal values and socialism. Nettlau stresses that with Bakunin three ideas interpenetrate in an organic fashion—atheism, and the necessity of free thought; socialism, the critique of capitalist exploitation; and anarchism, the negation of all forms of political coercion (the State)—thus consisting of "a living realization of freedom," liberty being the prime value of liberalism.[15]

To see the essence of Bakunin therefore in his Hegelian "idealism," or to see him a nihilist or an "extreme individualist," or to suggest that his ideas are simply a "restatement of Proudhon,"[16] or again, to imply that Bakunin was a latter-day Babeuf bent only on insurrectionary violence, is to put forward a very narrow and one-sided account of Bakunin's political philosophy. Pyziur is therefore essentially correct when he suggests that under the impact of Marxism, Bakunin developed an idea of anarchist communist order that is unique among his predecessors and contemporaries,[17] and thus deserves to be considered as an outstanding political theorist in his own right.

I shall give an account of Bakunin's political philosophy by considering his ideas under a number of headings, drawing extensively from Bakunin's own writings to illustrate his thought.

NOTES

1. Nettlau, M. 1976. *Writings on Bakunin*. London: C. Slienger, pp. 5-7.
2. Berlin, I. 1978. *Russian Thinkers*. Harmondsworth, Penguin, p. 83.
3. Berlin, op. cit., p. 108.
4. Berlin, op. cit., pp. 110-113.
5. Berlin, op. cit, p. 106.
6. Carr, E. H. 1937. *Michael Bakunin*, New York: Knopf, pp. 451-56.
7. Carr, op. cit., p. 175.
8. Maximoff, G. P., ed., 1953. *The Political Philosophy of Bakunin: Scientific Anarchism*. Glencoe: Free Press, pp. 21-22.
9. Avrich, P. 1988, *Anarchist Portraits*, Princeton, New Jersey: Princeton University Press,p. 6.
10. Pyziur, E. 1955. *The Doctrine of Anarchism of Michael Bakunin*, Milwaukee: Regnery, p. 16.
11. Carr, op. cit., p. 175.
12. Pyziur, op. cit., pp. 21-42.
13. Marx, K. & Engels, F. 1968. *Selected Works*, London: Lawrence & Wishort, p. 47.
14. Kramnick, I. 1972. "On Anarchism and the Real World: William Godwin and Radical England," *American Political Science Review*, 66, p. 128.
15. Nettlau, op. cit., p. 7.
16. Gray, A. 1946. *The Socialist Tradition: Moses to Lenin*. London: Longmans, p. 353.
17. Pyziur, op. cit., p. 41.

Chapter 9

Historical Materialism

B
AKUNIN'S conception of reality, like that of Marx's, is dialectical, materialist and deterministic. Like other nineteenth-century
theorists, Bakunin makes a distinction between two fundamentally contrasting approaches to reality, idealism and materialism, and
argues strongly that only a materialist approach is a valid one. He poses
the question in the extract subsequently published as *God and the State:*

> Who are right, the idealists or the materialists? The ques-
> tion once stated in this way, hesitation becomes impos-
> sible. Undoubtedly the idealists are wrong and the
> materialists are right. Yes facts are before ideas; yes, the
> ideal as Proudhon said, is but a flower, whose root lies in
> the material conditions of existence. Yes, the whole his-
> tory of humanity, intellectual and moral, political and so-
> cial, is but a reflection of its economic history.[1]

The social world, our humanity, is nothing other than the last and
supreme development—at least on our planet and as far as we know—
"the highest manifestation of animality." But Bakunin sees this as a
dialectical progression, the development of culture being the "gradual
negation of the animal element" in humans. Such development he sees
as both rational and natural, historical and logical. Drawing on the ideas
of Hegel and Comte, and aware of the developments in evolutionary
biology—Bakunin was writing only a decade after the publication of
Darwin's *Origin of Species*—Bakunin summed up the materialist outlook
as follows:

> One can clearly conceive the gradual development of the
> material world, as well as of organic life and of the his-
> torically progressive intelligence of man, individually
> and socially. It is an altogether natural movement, from
> the simple to the complex, from the lower to the higher,
> from the inferior to the superior; a movement in con-
> formity with all of our daily experiences and consequent-

ly in conformity also with our natural logic, with the distinctive laws of our mind, which, being formed and developed only through the aid of these same experiences are, so to speak, only its mental, cerebral reproduction or its recapitulation in thought.[2]

With this conception of reality as a kind of evolutionary process, and seeing human sociality and consciousness as a natural development, Bakunin denied any dualism between spirit and matter, humans and nature, which was intrinsic to the mechanistic philosophy of the Enlightenment. Being a part of nature, no rebellion against it by humans is possible: "Therefore man will never be able to combat Nature; he cannot conquer or master it." And he continues:

> Being the ultimate product of Nature on this earth, man, through his individual and social development, continues, so to speak, the work, creation, movement and life of Nature . . . Man's relations to this Universal Nature cannot be external, cannot be those of slavery or of struggle; he carries this Nature within himself and is nothing outside of it . . . It seems to me quite evident . . . that no revolt is possible on the part of man against what I call universal causality, or Universal Nature; the latter envelops and pervades man; it is within and outside of him, and it constitutes his whole being.[3]

It followed from this that everything in the world was in a sense determined or conditioned; the world was not chaotic, nor did humans have "free will" which Bakunin suggested was a theological concept:

> Nature, not withstanding the inexhaustible wealth and variety of beings of which it is constituted, does not by any means present chaos, but instead a magnificently organized world wherein every part is logically correlated to all the other parts," moreover, "all things are governed by inherent laws which constitute their own particular nature; that each thing has its own peculiar form of transformation and action.[4]

But Bakunin's notion of order was Hegelian. He saw it as a creative process rather than a mechanistic and static condition.

In Nature itself, that marvellous interrelationship and
network of phenomena is certainly not attained without
struggle. Quite the contrary, the harmony of the forces of
nature only appears as the actual result of that continual
struggle which is the very condition of life and movement . . . If order is natural and possible in the universe, it
is solely because this universe is not governed according
to some system imagined in advance and imposed by a
supreme will. Natural laws are inherent in nature, that is
to say they are not fixed by any authority. These laws are
only simple manifestations or else continual fluctuations
of the development of things and of combinations of
these very varied, transient but real facts.[5]

Like Spinoza and Godwin, Bakunin argues that as the human subject was essentially determined by the natural and social milieu, it was
futile to posit the notion of "free will" or to attribute a precise plan to
people's actions. Bakunin wrote:

Socialism, being founded upon positive science, absolutely rejects the doctrine of free will. It recognizes that
whatever is called human vice and virtue is absolutely the
product of the combined action of Nature and Society. All
individuals, with no exception, are at every moment of
their lives what Nature and Society have made them . . .
Hence it clearly follows that to make men moral it is necessary to make their social environment moral. And that can
be done in only one way; by assuring the triumph of justice, that is, the complete liberty of everyone in the most
perfect equality for all. Inequality of conditions and rights,
and the resulting lack of liberty for all, is the great collective iniquity begetting all individual iniquities.[6]

Many have seen Bakunin's stress on social and natural determinism
as completely incompatible with the emphasis he also makes on the free
human agent. But unless one thinks in terms of absolutes—something
which liberal critics of Bakunin continually accuse him of doing—then
there is no intrinsic incompatibility between freedom and necessity.
Another philosopher of freedom, Spinoza, is often criticized on these
same grounds. It seems, however, that it is the liberal critics themselves
who think in terms of absolutes and dualisms rather than Bakunin or

Spinoza. Bakunin makes it clear that liberty is not something absolute, nor is social determinism. He acknowledged that biological dispositions and attributes—physiological heredity—also had an influence on human behaviour.[7] He also placed, as we shall see, an important emphasis on the individual as a creative agent, both determining as well as being determined by natural and social conditions. The world itself in fact, was seen as a creative process. Bakunin therefore argued for a rational understanding of liberty, which denied the notion of free will— that is, "the presumed faculty of the human individual to determine himself freely and independently of any external influence"; such a notion of freedom, which removed humans from the principle of universal causality, Bakunin thought was nonsense. Two extracts will suffice to indicate his own understanding of the concept as something quite different from the metaphysical notion of free will.

> True, man, with the aid of knowledge and the thoughtful application of the laws of nature, gradually emancipates himself, but not from the universal yoke which he bears with all the living beings and the existing things that come into and disappear in this world. Man only frees himself from the brutal pressure exercised upon him by his own external world—material and social . . . Such is the only rational meaning of the word liberty; that is, the rule over external things, based upon the respectful observations of the laws of nature. It is independence from the pretensions and despotic acts from men; it is science, work, political revolt and along with all that, it is finally the well thought-out and free organization of the social environment in conformity with the natural laws inherent in every human society. The first and last condition of this liberty rests then on absolute submission to the omnipotence of nature.[8]

> The liberty of man consists solely in this; that he obeys natural laws because he has himself recognized them as such, and not because they have been externally imposed upon by an extrinsic will whatever, divine or human, collective or individual.[9]

Bakunin thus came to contrast a materialist approach, with its emphasis on natural causality and freedom, with metaphysical idealism.

The latter approach, instead of "wisely accompanying the progressive and real movement from the world called inorganic to the world organic, vegetable animal and then distinctly human,"[10] begins with God, conceptualized either as a person or divine substance. Following Comte he sees religion and idealist metaphysics in historical terms, as an earlier form of human understanding. "The first thinkers," he wrote "were necessarily theologians and metaphysicians." And he posits materialism (positive science) and idealism (religious metaphysics) as two contrasting forms of understanding. He sums up the contrast in the following words:

> Materialism starts from animality to establish humanity; idealism starts with divinity to establish slavery and to condemn the masses to perpetual animality. Materialism denies free will and ends in the establishment of liberty; idealism in the name of human dignity, proclaims free will, and, on the ruins of every liberty, founds authority; materialism rejects the principle of authority, because it rightly considers it the corollary of animality, and because on the contrary, the triumph of humanity which is the object and chief significance of history, can be realized only through liberty.[11]

In Hegelian fashion, Bakunin sees human history as a world process, as the progressive move towards greater freedom, first with the development of life, then, with human culture and consciousness, humans establish a degree of autonomy from the world of nature, finally, with the potential establishment of a truly human society, the freedom of the individual. Human freedom for Bakunin can only be in nature and society, not something independent from the world.

He poses the question as to why religion and the belief in God came into being. Since humans are at one with Nature and are essentially material beings, how did this duality—of spirit (divinity) and nature—come into being, and take such a deep root in human consciousness.[12] Drawing on the ideas of Spinoza, Feuerbach and the left-Hegelians, Bakunin offers many tentative suggestions: religion is related to fear and insecurity; it is the first awakening of human reason, "the first gleam of human truth through the divine veil of falsehood" — the use of the faculty of abstraction to understand the world; it reflects a "deep discontent"—an instinctive and passionate protest against the wretchedness of much human existence. He does not deny that religion may have been a "historic necessity" and does not wish to affirm that it has always been an "absolute evil" in human history,[13] nevertheless, Bakunin's essential attitude to religion, and to metaphysical philosophy generally, is a critical one. He sees it, like Freud and Marx, as limiting human capacity for reason and free-thinking and as bolstering hierarchical structures and despotic regimes. We have noted earlier Bakunin's thoughts on the Paris Commune and on Mazzini's defence of religion.

Bakunin implies, with Feuerbach, that God (religion) is but a "mirage," one in which humans, through faith or ignorance, discover their own image, but in an inverted-divinized-fashion. "God being everything, the real world and man are nothing. God being truth, justice, goodness, beauty, power and life, man is falsehood, iniquity, evil, ugliness, impotence and death. God being master, man is slave." And he continues in famous, oft-quoted phrases:

> The idea of God implies the abdication of human reason and justice; it is the most decisive negation of known liberty, and necessarily ends in the enslavement of mankind, both in theory and practice . . . he who desires to worship God must harbour no childish illusions about the matter, but bravely renounce his liberty and humanity.
>
> If God is, man is a slave; now man can and must be free; then, God does not exist.
>
> I defy anyone whosoever to avoid this circle.[14]

There have been some anarchists who have continued to believe in God, but have interpreted the latter concept either in terms of the human spirit or, have taken great care, as Bakunin hinted, not to give any positive definition of divinity at all. They use it as a "generic name of all that seems grand, good, beautiful, noble, human to them." Bakunin concluded that "If God really existed, it would be necessary to abolish him."[15]

Bakunin had some very harsh things to say about religion: it debased and corrupted people, it was cruel and based on the key ritual of sacrifice; it dishonoured human labour; it supported privilege and despotism; it was a key obstacle to the emancipation of society in hampering human reason. It had helped humans to make the "first step towards humanity," but now it was a hindrance and fetter to full human emancipation. As with Marx and other materialist scholars, Bakunin was a firm believer in social evolution, and held that "the subsequent progressive development of various theologies can be explained naturally as the reflection of the development of humanity in history."[16] It thus follows that free-thought propaganda, though useful in itself, would not eradicate religion, for people go to church, as they go to the pothouse (pub), to alleviate their misery. "Give them a human existence and they will never go into a pot-house or church. And it is only the Social Revolution that can and shall give them such an existence."[17] The socialist historian, Alexander Gray, suggests that it might be a useful exercise for theological students to require them to write a reasoned refutation of Bakunin's writings on religion.[18] No refutation has ever been forthcoming from this or any other quarter.

Bakunin's philosophical writings on Nature present in embryonic form, an ecological approach to the world, one that is materialist and historical, and stresses the essential continuity and organic link between humans and nature. But Bakunin seems to have had very much an urban aesthetic feeling towards nature, in contrast to his two anarchist "disciples" who were to make, towards the end of the nineteenth century, important contributions to ecological theory—Elisée Reclus and Peter Kropotkin. Bakunin's contributions to sociology, however, were much more significant, indeed they were profound, for he offered important insights into the sociality of the human species, insights that anticipate the theories of many pragmatists, existentialists and social scientists writing more than fifty years later.

NOTES

1. Lehning, A. 1973. *Michael Bakunin: Selected Writings*. London: Cape, p. 111.
2. Maximoff, G. P. 1953. ed., *The Political Philosophy of Bakunin: Scientific Anarchism*. Glencoe: Free Press, p. 175.
3. Maximoff, op. cit., p. 91.
4. Maximoff, op. cit., pp. 54-55.
5. Lehning, op. cit., p. 208.
6. Maximoff, op. cit., p. 155.
7. Maximoff, op. cit., p. 154.
8. Maximoff, op. cit., p. 96.
9. Lehning, op. cit., p. 130.
10. Lehning, op. cit., p. 116.
11. Maximoff, op. cit., p. 173.
12. Maximoff, op. cit., p. 106.
13. Maximoff, op. cit., p. 116.
14. Lehning, op. cit., p. 125.
15. Lehning, op. cit., pp. 127-128.
16. Maximoff, op. cit., p. 115.
17. Maximoff, op. cit., p. 120.
18. Gray, A. 1946. *The Socialist Tradition: Moses to Lenin*, London: Longmans, p. 356.

Chapter 10

Social Philosophy

Organic life, having begun with the simplest, hardly organized cell, and having led it through the whole range of transformation—from the organization of plant life to that of animal life— has finally made man out of it.[1]

FOR Bakunin, human beings, like everything else in nature, are entirely material beings, and the mind, the thinking faculty with the power to receive and reflect on different external and internal sensation, is the property of an animal body. As with all animals, humans, Bakunin writes, have two essential instincts or drives: egoism, the instinct for self-preservation, and the social instinct which is ultimately concerned with the preservation of the species.[2] What is called society or the human world has no other creator that the human species who is impelled, as are other living creatures, by a force or instinctive will within the organism. Bakunin refers to this as the "universal life current" and associates it with "universal causality"—thus suggesting that by natural laws, Bakunin meant something closer to Freud's libido or Tao, rather than "mechanistic laws."[3] Bakunin's writings on the will, clearly derived from Schopenhauer (whom he read with interest in his last years though he was critical of the philosopher's individualism) have a biological rather than a moral import (as with Kant) and, as with Nietzsche, evidently anticipate Freud.

Bakunin also stresses the fundamental importance of work in the constitution of the human subject:

> Every animal works; or lives by working Man as a living being, which is the supreme law of life. He must work in order to maintain existence, in order to develop in the fullness of his being.[4]

And Bakunin emphasizes that human work has a progressive quality.

Bakunin goes on to suggest that three fundamental principles constitute the essential conditions of all human development: 1) human animality, the "material" aspects of the human subject discussed above;

2) human thought, which represents a "new element" in the historical process, and 3) rebellion. Thought and rebellion are seen as two faculties that combine the "progressive action throughout the history of mankind and consequently create all which constitutes humanity in man."[5] Bakunin recounts the Genesis myth where Jehovah expressly forbids Adam and Eve from touching the fruit of the tree of knowledge. "But here steps in Satan, the eternal rebel, the first freethinker and the emancipator of worlds. He makes man ashamed of his bestial ignorance and obedience, he emancipates him and stamps upon his brow the seal of liberty and humanity, in urging him to disobey and eat the fruit of knowledge."[6] Thus, rebellion, human emancipation and knowledge are seen as intrinsically linked by Bakunin. In his study "Beyond the Chains of Illusion," Erich Fromm notes how in Greek and Hebrew myths the capacity for disobedience constituted the beginning of human history,[7] yet he makes no mention of Bakunin.

But the most important insights of Bakunin relate to his discussions on the essential social nature of the human subject, and on his postulate that human freedom and rationality are intrinsically bound-up in society. These discussions are closely linked to his critique of Jean-Jacques Rousseau, a critique that has been lost on many liberal scholars who still largely continue to see the subject in asocial terms.

In his address to the League for Peace and Freedom, entitled "Federalism, Socialism and Anti-Theologism" (1867), Bakunin concluded the proposal with a long diatribe against Rousseau's theory of the State. He was concerned that Rousseau's democratic theory was not only a justification for the State, but made human freedom and sociality into rigid antithetical concepts. We can trace his argument against Rousseau's "social contract" theory by quoting some relevant extracts. Bakunin writes:

> Man is not only the most individual being on earth, but also the most social. Jean-Jacques Rousseau was surely mistaken in his belief that primitive society was established by a free contract, effected by savages. But Rousseau is not alone in his assertion. The majority of modern jurists and publicists, whether of the Kantian or any other individualist liberal school ... take the tacit contract as their point of departure. A tacit contract ... What terrible nonsense! An absurd and, worse, a pernicious fiction!
>
> The implications of the social contract are in fact fatal, because they culminate in the absolute domination

of the State. And yet the principle seems extremely liberal at first sight. Before arranging their contract, individuals are assumed to have enjoyed absolute liberty, because this theory holds that only man in his natural, wild State is totally free . . .

So here we have primitive men, each one totally free . . . enjoying his freedom only as long as he does not come into contact with another and remains immersed in absolute individual isolation . . . In order not to utterly destroy one another, they form an explicit or tacit contract by which they relinquish a part of themselves so as to safeguard the rest. This contract becomes the basis of society, or rather of the State, for it must be noted that there is no room in the theory for society, only for the State, or rather that society is totally absorbed by the State.[8]

And Bakunin continues by making an important distinction between society and State, earlier made by both Tom Paine and Godwin:

Society is the natural medium of the human collectivity, regardless of contracts. It progresses slowly, through the momentum imparted by individual initiatives, not through the mind and will of the legislator. There may be many unarticulated laws that rule it, but these are natural laws, inherent in the social body . . . If it follows that they are not to be confused with the judicial and political laws proclaimed by some legislative authority.[9]

Bakunin goes on to suggest that individual liberty ends where the State begins, and that it is "the most flagrant, the most cynical, the most complete negation of humanity."[10] He then develops a critique of the State, which we will discuss further in a later section.

In his study "The Krouto-Germanic Empire and the Social Revolution" Bakunin takes up again the critique of those he calls "doctrinaire liberals" and the "individualist, egoist, base and fraudulent liberty extolled by the school of Jean-Jacques Rousseau and every other bourgeois liberalism."[11] According to these liberals—who don't hesitate to support a coercive State when it serves their interests—

. . . the freedom of the individual is not a creation, an historical product of society. They claim that it is previous to

any society, and that every man bears it from birth on-
wards, together with his immortal soul, as a divine gift. It
follows that only outside of society is man complete . . .

What emerges from this theory is that our society
proper does not exist; it utterly ignores natural human
society, the real starting point of all human civilization
and the only medium in which the personality and liberty
of man can really be born and grow. All it acknowledges
is, at one extreme, the individual . . . and at the other the
State. (Liberals are well aware that no historic State has
ever been based on a contract, and that they have all been
founded by violence and conquest. But they need this fiction of the free contract as the basis of the State, so they
grasp it without further ado.[12]

Against this liberal conception of the individual, which sees a fundamental antithesis between the free individual and society (State)—
which Bakunin suggests is essentially an idealist theory—Bakunin
outlines his own materialist theory. This he postulates in ways much
more enlightening than either Hegel or Marx, or the later Durkheim,
that is, he stresses the fundamentally social nature of the human subject. Bakunin writes:

Society, preceding in time any development of humanity
constitutes the very essence of human existence. Man is
born into society, just as an ant is born into an ant-hill or a
bee into its hive; man is born into society from the very
moment that he becomes a human being, that is, a being
possessing to a greater or lesser extent the power of
speech and thought. Man does not choose society; on the
contrary he is the product of the latter. . . .[13]

Society is the basis and natural starting point of man's
human existence, and it follows that he only realizes his
individual liberty or personality by integration with all
the individuals around him and by virtue of the collective
power of society. According to the materialist theory . . . instead of diminishing or constricting the freedom of the individual, society creates it. Society is the root and branch,
liberty the fruit. Therefore, in every era man must find his
liberty, not at the beginning, but at the ends of history, and
it may be said that the real and total emancipation of every

human individual is the true great objective and ultimate goal of history.[14]

And Bakunin continues:

> The materialist ... definition of liberty flatly contradicts the idealists. It is as follows: Man does not become man, nor does he achieve awareness or realization of his humanity, other than in society and in the collective movement of the whole society; he only shakes off the yoke of internal nature through collective or social labour ... and without his material emancipation there can be no intellectual or moral emancipation for anyone ... man in isolation can have no awareness of his liberty. Being free for man means being acknowledged, considered and treated as such by another man, and by all the men around him. Liberty is therefore a feature not of isolation but of interaction, not of exclusion but rather of connection ... I myself am human and free only to the extent that I acknowledge the humanity and liberty of all my fellows ... I am properly free when all the men and women about me are equally free. Far from being a limitation or a denial of my liberty, the liberty of another is its necessary condition and confirmation.[15]

Isaiah Berlin refers to all this as "glib Hegelian claptrap" and one of his devotees concurs, referring to Bakunin's "extraordinary abstract ideal of liberty."[16] But Bakunin's concept of liberty is not abstract at all, rather concrete, suggesting that human freedom only has meaning within a social context and, moreover, as we shall see, can be meaningful only in a society which not only acknowledges personal freedom but has as a degree of economic equity that makes such liberty possible. Bakunin's critique of Rousseau has gone unheeded by most liberals, who themselves have a far more abstract conception of liberty, happily acknowledging it even in the context of the State and rampant economic exploitation.

A number of interesting points emerge from Bakunin's discussion. First, Bakunin makes it clear that the religious idea that one can achieve freedom or salvation outside society—as with mystics or anchorite saints—is misconceived. The notion of a solitary and abstract individual is just as much an abstraction as is God, he writes, and to become concerned with the liberty inherent in the divine soul is to become anti-so-

cial. Life outside of society, outside of all known influences, "a life of absolute isolation, is tantamount to intellectual, moral and material
death."[17]

Second, Bakunin postulated not only a negative conception of liberty—consisting of rebellion against all forms of authority—but also a
positive conception of liberty. (Berlin and Fromm also wrote about two
forms of liberty without ever acknowledging Bakunin.) The positive
concept of liberty, which Bakunin conceived as "an eminently social
matter," he defined as follows: "It is the full development and full enjoyment of all human faculties and powers in every man, through upbringing, scientific education, and material prosperity."[18] He speaks too of the
only freedom truly worthy of the name—"the freedom which consists in
the full development of all the material, intellectual and moral power
which are found in the form of latent capabilities in every individual. I
mean that freedom which recognizes only those restrictions which are
laid down for us by the laws of our own nature . . . Thus, instead of
trying to find a limit for them, we should consider them as the real conditions of and the real reason for our freedom"[19]—this in response to
Rousseau. Elsewhere he writes of the need to proclaim anew the great
principles of the French revolution; that every person should have the
material and moral means to develop his whole humanity. The principle
he suggests must be translated into a problem:

> To organize society, in such a manner that every in-
> dividual, man or woman, should, at birth, find almost
> equal means for the development of his or her various
> faculties and the full utilization of his or her work.[20]

Aileen Kelly suggests that Bakunin's "own need to achieve self-
realization as a real or integrated personality" was the key to his personality,[21] but completely ignores the fact that self-actualization—the full
development of the individual—was Bakunin's own conception of positive liberty. Other writers from Jung to Maslow have posited "self-actualization" as a crucial need or drive of the human personality, although
this has largely been theorized, as Russell Jacoby (1975) notes, within a
context of "social amnesia." Bakunin, unlike these humanistic
psychologists, was fully aware that positive liberty—"self-realization"—
was only possible in a society where people were not subject to coercive
constraints and economic exploitation. Kelly's suggestion[22] that
"freedom" and "equality" for Bakunin were simply "fine-sounding ethical categories" and that his writings lack any "serious analysis of social

and political questions" (she accepts the warped opinion of Engels), is just perverse. Her own study is somewhat pathetic in that she nowhere seriously engages herself in Bakunin's own critique of liberal ideology, the State, capitalism, and Marxism—all real social and political issues.

Third, Bakunin argues that while the State is in a sense artificial and can be eliminated, society is the natural medium for the human subject and cannot be rebelled against. He writes:

> Society antedates and at the same time survives every human individual, beings in this respect like Nature itself. It's eternal like Nature, or rather, having been born upon our earth, it will last as long as the earth. A radical revolt against society would therefore be just as impossible for man as a revolt against nature, human society being nothing else but the last great manifestation or creation of Nature upon this earth. And an individual who would want to rebel against society . . . would play himself beyond the pole of existence.[23]

And Bakunin suggests that while an individual may well react against society, especially when influenced "by feelings coming from outside and especially from an alien society, but the individual cannot leave this particular society without immediately placing himself in another sphere of solidarity and without becoming subjected to new influences."[24]

Some writers have inferred from this that while Bakunin was hostile to the State he was quite happy to allow social pressure in the form of public opinion. Gray, for instance, writes that while Bakunin was delivering us from a visible tyranny (the State) he may be subjecting the human race to an even more "grievous tyranny"—public opinion.[25] On this issue Bakunin writes:

> Social tyranny is often overwhelming and deadly, but it does not exhibit the character of imperative violence, of legalized, formal despotism, which distinguishes State authority . . . it exerts its domination by means of conventions, morals, and a multitude of sentiments, prejudices and habits, in the material as well as the mental sphere and constitutes what we call public opinion. It envelops man from the moment of his birth . . . hence the immense power which society exercises over men.

But Bakunin continues,

> ... this power may be just as much beneficial as harmful.
> It is beneficial when it contributes to the development of
> knowledge, material prosperity, liberty, equality and
> brotherly solidarity, harmful when it had opposite ten-
> dencies.[26]

Bakunin all his life was concerned with an attempt to outline the
kind of society that was conducive to human liberty and solidarity—a
truly human society. It was one that was both socialist and libertarian
and no one, as far as I am aware, has improved much on Bakunin's essential ideas. All contemporary societies are characterized—if liberals
like Kelly removed their tinted glasses—by violence, poverty, repression, pollution and plunder, and the theoretical alternatives to social
anarchism—orthodox communism, liberal democracy and fascism—
are all morally and politically bankrupt.

Finally, something needs to be said on how Bakunin saw the
relationship between the individual and society, for he has been accused both of being an "extreme individualist" and an extreme "collectivist," completely "submerging" the individual in the collectivity.
Marxists tend to stress individualism—Marx accused Bakunin of merely translating "Proudhon's and Stirner's anarchy into the crude language of the tartars"[27]—while liberals stress his supposed collectivism.
Both interpretations are grossly unjust to Bakunin—indeed wilful.

The extracts above should make it clear that Bakunin saw the human
subject as an essentially social being, and found no justification for the
society/individual opposition. His stress on rebellion, individuality, and
liberty was always counterpoised with an equal stress on sociality and
human social solidarity. One of the most perceptive of socialist historians,
G. D. H. Cole, sums up well Bakunin's social philosophy:

> Bakunin's social theory began, and almost ended, with
> liberty. Against the claims of liberty nothing else in his
> view was worth consideration at all. He attacked, remor-
> selessly and without qualification, every institution that
> seem to him to be inconsistent with liberty ... Yet he was
> very far from being an individualist, and he had the most
> utmost scorn for the kinds of liberty that were preached
> by the bourgeois advocates of laissez-faire. He was, or
> believed himself to be, a socialist as well as a libertarian,

and no one has insisted more strongly than he on the evils of private property and of the competition of man with man. When he wrote about the nature of society he always laid emphasis on the immense impact of social environment on the individual, stressing fully as much as Durkheim the social origin . . . of men's ideas.[28]

The "collectivist" orientation of Bakunin's thought had been proposed by Aileen Kelly, who, like Berlin and Carr, tends to see these ideas as having totalitarian implications. Bakunin, she argues, was centrally concerned with "wholeness," and with that "eschatological vision of a unified human community" in which the individual is "submerged." She writes:

For Bakunin, liberty was above all "wholeness": the dialectical overcoming of all duality, all conflict between subject and object, the part and the whole, in a unity with the Absolute which was at one and the same time the infinite self-assertion and the total dissolution of the individual ego.[29]

Bakunin was thus a kind of mystic, but a romantic mystic who found his absolute in the popular masses—the people. Such a thesis makes nonsense even of Hegel whose dialectic was one of "unity-in-opposition," not of mystical "union"—the "identity" theory of religious mystics and Schelling which Hegel indeed derided. As he put it in the "Phenomenology" this to palm off the Absolute as the night in which all cows are black. Hegel was concerned with advancing a concrete metaphysics and overcoming dualisms—but not by collapsing or "dissolving" the oppositions. As an interpretation of Bakunin's social philosophy it is even more perverse, for unlike Kelly, Bakunin had a good understanding not only of Hegelian idealism, but of the emerging sciences of sociology and anthropology. The influence of Comte is evident in much of his work, and he was a close friend of two important early anthropologists/geographers, Eliseé and Elie Reclus, as Cole rightly points out.[30]

Although one may find occasional thoughts about the need for a revolutionary to identify him or herself with the people, it is patently clear from Bakunin's writings that he saw the relationship between the individual and society as a "dialectical" one and being dialectic means that it is a unity-in-opposition, and also one of movement and change.

Bakunin saw all relationships both in nature and society, as being in a state of flux. The relationship between the individual and the collective is neither collapsed nor equated, nor is it seen in rigid dualistic terms. Bakunin's whole project was to delineate a society in which both liberty and sociality were safeguarded. Kelly's assertion that Bakunin resolved the fundamental problem of ethics and political theory—the relationship between liberty and equality as a conflicting goal—with the "stroke of a pen," considering them as one and the same thing,[31] indicates a woeful misunderstanding of Bakunin's argument. He did not—as we shall see—equate them or consider them as in inherent conflict; he argues that economic equality was a basic condition for liberty. Only supporters of capitalism see equality in conflict with liberty.

But Kelly does Bakunin a further injustice. Not only does she link Bakunin's theory to a misreading of Hegel's idealism, thus seeing him involved in "quasi-religious ecstasy" looking forward to "the dissolution of the personality in a collective,"[32] she also follows Isaiah Berlin in unfairly foisting upon Bakunin a Jacobin conception of politics. She writes:

> Given that the use of force is the only way yet devised of eliminating tension between the individual and the whole, the proponents of the ideal of the unity of civil and political society are constrained by their own logic to propose a dictatorship which submerges the first in the second as a means to the goal of the ideal society.[33]

This may be an apt description of the kind of politics associated with Rousseau, Robespierre and Stalin, but to see it as characterizing Bakunin's conception of the revolution and of anarchy is either political naivety or indicates an astonishing aberration of scholarship.

In a more systematic liberal appraisal of Bakunin, E. Lampert has stressed that an emphasis on the autonomy and freedom of the individual subject co-exists in Bakunin with a stress on human sociality. Bakunin, he writes, through emphasizing the primacy of society over the individual, never "professed the belief in an illusory, hypostatized collective consciousness" and consistently spurned any notion of attachment to something outside man. Even at his most collectivist, Bakunin always emphasizes the revolt of the human personality against all powers, collective or divine. But Bakunin could equally not be described as an "individualist," for all the operations in the life of an individual—liberty, consciousness, reason—had for Bakunin social meaning. And so Bakunin differed fundamentally from the other radical anarchist, Max Stirner.[34]

NOTES

1. Maximoff, G. P. 1953. ed., *The Political Philosophy of Bakunin: Scientific Anarchism.* Glencoe: Free Press, p. 84.
2. Maximoff, op. cit., p. 146.
3. Maximoff, op. cit., p. 95.
4. Maximoff, op. cit., pp. 87-88.
5. Maximoff, op. cit., p. 84.
6. Lehning, A. 1973. *Michael Bakunin: Selected Writings.* London: Cape, p. 112.
7. Fromm, E. 1962. *Beyond the Chains of Illusion,* London: Sphere Books, p. 158.
8. Lehning, op. cit., pp. 136-37.
9. Lehning, op. cit., pp. 136-37.
10. Dolgoff, S. 1973. ed., trans, introd. *Bakunin on Anarchy.* New York: Knopf, p. 133.
11. Dolgoff, op. cit., p. 261.
12. Lehning, op. cit., pp. 140-141.
13. Maximoff, op. cit., p. 157.
14. Lehning, op. cit., p. 145.
15. Lehning, op. cit., pp. 146-148.
16. Kelly, A. 1982. *Mikhail Bakunin: A Study in the Psychology and Politics of Utopianism.* Oxford: Clarendon Press, p. 198.
17. Maximoff, op. cit., p. 169.
18. Lehning, op. cit., p. 149.
19. Lehning, op. cit., p. 196.
20. Maximoff, op. cit., p. 156.
21. Kelly, op. cit., p. 97.
22. Kelly, op. cit., p. 199.
23. Maximoff, op. cit., p. 144.
24. Maximoff, op. cit. pp. 168-69.
25. Gray, A. 1946. *The Socialist Tradition: Moses to Lenin.* London: Longmans, p. 362.
26. Lehning, op. cit., p. 150.
27. Marx, K. et al. 1972 *Anarchism and Anarcho-Syndicalism.* Moscow: Progress Publishers, p. 152.
28. Cole, G.D.H., 1954. *History of Socialist Thought, Vol. II, Marxism and Anarchism 1850-1890.* London: Macmillan, p. 219.
29. Kelly, op. cit., p. 194.
30. Cole, op. cit., p. 222.
31. Kelly, op. cit., p. 197.
32. Kelly, op. cit., p. 255.
33. Kelly, op. cit., p. 292.
34. Lampert, E. 1957. *Studies in Rebellion.* London: Routledge & Kegan Paul, pp. 160-61.

Chapter 11

Critique of the State

W HAT is freedom? What is slavery? Bakunin asks. And he answers:

> Does man's freedom consist in revolting against all laws?
> We say No, in so far as laws are natural, economic, and
> social laws, not authoritatively imposed, but inherent in
> things, in relations, in situations, in natural development
> of which is expressed by those laws. We say Yes, if there
> are political and juridical laws, imposed by men upon
> men; whether violently by the right of force; whether by
> deceit and hypocrisy—in the name of religion or any
> doctrine whatever; or finally, by the dint of the fiction,
> the democratic falsehood called universal suffrage.[1]

Bakunin was critical of all aspects of the existing order that
restricted human liberty, and his critique largely focused around three
institutions—the State, religion and capitalism. Like other anarchists,
Bakunin saw the State, in all forms, as one of the most fundamental
manifestations of domination, and a critique of the State permeates all
his writings. He sees the State as the antithesis of liberty, human well-
being and morality. Such a critique was insistent and uncompromising.
In his major study, *The Knouto-Germanic Empire and the Social Revolution*,
Bakunin continually draws a distinction between society, the essential
medium and context of human well-being and liberty, and the State.
There is no point in asking, he writes, whether social life is good or evil,
it has a real existence like the natural world, and is necessary for human
life. We cannot step outside of society; we can only try to create the
right kind of social conditions that are conducive to liberty and to
human solidarity and well-being. But:

> The State is another matter, and I have no hesitation in
> saying that the State is evil, but a historically necessary
> evil, as necessary in the past as its utter extinction will

eventually become in the future . . . The State is not a society, but one of its historical forms, at once brutish and abstract. Historically, it was born out of the marriage of violence, rapine and plunder—in other words, of war and conquest . . . From its beginning it has been the divine mainstay of brute force and rampant injustice. Even in the most democratic lands, such as the United States of America and Switzerland, it is the prevailing (sanction) of minority privilege and the practical subjugation of the vast majority.[2]

Bakunin therefore advances a historical theory of the origins of the State—one of the first formulations of the "conquest" theory of the State. At the turn of the century, this theory was given its fullest expression by the German sociologist, Franz Oppenheimer, in his classic study *The State* (1914). Bakunin's theory was therefore very different—and much less abstract—than the two other prevailing nineteenth-century theories of the State—the absolutist and social contract theories. Bakunin writes of these:

According to liberal political writers, the first State was created by man's free and conscious will; according to the Absolutists, the State is a divine creation.[3]

Neither theory had any historical substance. But both theories tend to suggest, Bakunin writes, that the "state dominates society and tends together to absorb it." In Absolutist theory, the State, as a divine institution, totally absorbs the natural associations, while social contract theorists virtually deny the very existence of society.[4] Bakunin is naturally critical of both theories.

Bakunin's critique of the State has many different facets. He denies in fact that under coercive structures liberty and well-being can be possible. While stressing the importance of society he simultaneously rejects the State. Outside of society, he writes, "man would not only not be free, but he would not be transformed into a real man at all, that is to say, into a being who has self-consciousness, who alone thinks and speaks."[5] But the State is an "abstraction" that is antithetical to liberty and humanity. He writes:

It is clear that freedom will never be given to mankind, and that the real interests of society, of all the groups and

local associations as well as of all the individuals who
make up society, will only be able to find real satisfaction
when there are no more States. It is clear that all the so-
called general interests of society, which the State is alleged to represent and which in reality are nothing but
the constant and general negation of the positive interests of the regions, communes, associations and the
largest number of individuals subjected to the State, constitute an abstraction, a fiction, a lie, and that the State is
one great slaughterhouse, and like an immense
graveyard and where . . . all the living initiatives of a nation (are) sanctimoniously sacrificed and buried.[6]

He thus likens the State to a "vast cemetery" wherein all manifestations of individual and local life are sacrificed. "It is the altar on which
the real liberty and the well-being of people are immolated to political
grandeur." The State therefore is seen by Bakunin not as "a natural
human society which supports and reinforces the life of everyone by
the life of all—quite the contrary, it is the immolation of every individual as well as of local associations, it is an abstraction which is
destructive to a living society."[7] For Bakunin it is the nature of the State
to disrupt human solidarity, to restrict liberty, and thus "in a sense to
deny humanity."[8]

Bakunin examines the arguments of both the Jacobins and the
liberal democrats wherein the State represents the common interests of
a society. He rejects these arguments fervently.

It will be argued that the State, the representative of the
public weal or of the interest common to all, curtails a
part of everyone's liberty in order to assure the
remainder of this liberty. But this remainder is security, if
you please, yet it is by no means liberty. For liberty is in-
divisible; a part of it cannot be curtailed without destroying it as a whole.[9]

The positive interests of society are represented by local associations, communes and individuals, Bakunin argues, not by the State,
and the so-called "general interests" of society constitute "an abstraction, a fiction, a falsehood." If society as a whole, in order to constitute
itself as such, "demands the sacrifice of individuals and local interests,
how then can it in reality represent them in their totality?[10]

The historical reality of the State is quite different, and it is ironic that liberal political commentators who chide Bakunin for being purely concerned with "abstractions" should spend so much time themselves writing about the political "abstractions" of Plato, Rousseau, Locke and Hegel! The reality of the "State" for Bakunin is its support for privilege and inequality, and its fundamental basis in coercive violence. He writes:

> What do we see throughout history? The State has always been the patrimony of some privileged class: the sacerdotal class, the nobility, the bourgeoisie—and finally, when all the other classes have exhausted themselves, the class of bureaucracy enters upon the stage and then the State falls, or rises, if you please, to the position of a machine.[11]

The State in its contemporary form is intrinsically connected with capitalism, Bakunin suggests. "Modern capitalist production and banking speculations demand for their full development a vast centralized State apparatus which alone is capable of subjecting the millions of toilers to their exploitation."[12] And capitalism can happily co-exist with a representative democracy. But rather than highlighting the differences in State forms, Bakunin puts a central emphasis on what they all have in common—domination and the upholding of privilege.

> The State, any State—even when it dresses-up in the most liberal and democratic form—is necessarily based upon domination, and upon violence, that is, upon despotism—a concealed but no less dangerous despotism . . . The State, or political right, denotes force, authority, predominance; it presupposes inequality, in fact. Where all rule, there are no more rules, but there is no State. Where all equally enjoy the same human rights, then all political right loses its reason for being.[13]

Such notions as "equality of political rights" or the "democratic State" are thus, for Bakunin, contradictions in terms. If the term "democracy" denoted government of the people, by the people, for the people, then this would imply no State, and Bakunin could therefore happily call himself a "democrat." But a representative democracy based on universal suffrage was quite a different institution, and

Bakunin was highly critical of what this entailed in reality. His writings on this are seminal and cogent, and have still not been taken on board by liberal theorists, most of whom seem unable to imagine modern society without State structures. Some of Bakunin's writings on this issue are worth quoting:

> But, we are told, the democratic State, based upon free universal suffrage for all its citizens, surely cannot be the negation of their liberty. And why not? This depends absolutely upon the mission and the power which the citizens delegate to the State. And a republican State, based upon universal suffrage, could be exceedingly despotic, even more despotic than a monarchic State, when under the pretext of representing the will of everyone, it bears down upon the will and the free movement of everyone of its members with the whole weight of its collective power...
>
> I frankly confess that I do not share the superstitious devotion of your bourgeois radicals and your republican bourgeois to universal suffrage. So long as universal suffrage is exercised in a society where the people, the masses of workers, are economically dominated by a minority holding in exclusive possession the property and capital of the country, free of independent thought the people may be otherwise, or as they appear to be from a political aspect, these elections held under conditions of universal suffrage can only be illusionary, anti-democratic in their results, which invariably will prove to be absolutely opposed to the needs, instincts and real will of the population.[14]

Bakunin's writings are infused with a historical sense, and his criticisms are backed with empirical observations regarding the nature of the contemporary States. Like Proudhon, he observed that universal suffrage in the wake of the 1848 revolution led to reaction. Did not, he asks, the plebiscite after the *coup d'état* of December 1851 yield seven million "yes" votes to the Emperor who then established himself as a practical dictator of France? He quotes the phrase "Universal Suffrage is Counter-Revolutionary."[15] He also notes that the establishment of universal suffrage turns out to be something of a "great illusion" and a "fraud." These democratic States still involve the rule of a privileged few and the oppression of the majority of the populations. Universal suffrage, Bakunin wrote:

> . . . does not prevent the formations of a body of politicians, privileged in fact though not in law, who, devoting themselves exclusively to the adminstration of the nations's public affairs, end by forming a sort of political aristocracy or oligarchy, as can be seen by the example of Switzerland and of the United States of America.[16]

And such oligarchies are intrinsically linked by Bakunin to the maintenance of capitalist inequalities.

For Bakunin, individual liberty and the State, freedom and power, are mutually exclusive. "Every government, even the most democratic one, is the natural enemy of freedom, and the stronger it is, the more concentrated its power, the more oppressive it becomes." It is not remarkable, he wrote, that it was a republican who was destined to play the first basis for the military dictatorship in Europe, that it was Robespierre who paved the road for the State despotism personified by Napoleon. Capitalist monopoly has always and everywhere been accompanied by the intensification and extension of State Power. In two revolutions the French lost their freedoms, seeing a democratic republic turned into a military dictatorship. On the French revolution Bakunin concluded:

> Thus, this Revolution, which at first was inspired by love for liberty and humanity, only because it came to believe in the possibility of reconciling these two concepts with State centralization, committed suicide, and killed both, begetting in their place only a military dictatorship, Caesarism.[17]

Bakunin also stressed the fact that in times of political crisis the true colours of the republican bourgeoisie invariably showed themselves. They then became the most passionate and rabid enemies of a social revolution and supporters of the State, for they realize that it is only through the State that the right of the propertied classes to exploit the labour of the propertyless majority is guaranteed.[18]

Bakunin's conclusion therefore is that "the very existence of the State demands that there be some privileged class virtually interested in maintaining that existence"[19] and that the distinction between the various forms of government—monarchy, military, bureaucratic and republican—is in their form rather than in their substance.

> The State denotes violence, oppression, exploitation and injustice raised into a system and made into the cornerstone of any society . . . The State is the complete negation of humanity . . . the opposite of human freedom and justice, and the violent breach of the universal solidarity of the human race . . . All States are bad in the sense that by their very nature, that is, by conditions and objectives of their existence, they constitute the very opposite of human justice, freedom and equality.[20]

For Bakunin, there wasn't much to choose between the Russian autocratic Empire and the representative democracies of Britain and Switzerland. Despotism resides not so much in "the form of the State or power as in the very principle of the State or political power."[21]

People generally have, Bakunin suggests, two basic needs; material well being and liberty. States are a direct negation of these, but they are also intrinsically linked by Bakunin to two other institutions that are detrimental to human freedom—the church and capitalism. Bakunin, as many have suggested, saw God and the State in very similar terms. His revolt against God (or at least the idea of God) and his rejection of the State are but two aspects of his concern for any arbitrary limitation of human liberty. The political abstraction of the State was "God's earthly complement." Bakunin writes in a significant passage:

> To prove the identity of the State and church, I shall ask the reader to take note of the fact that both are essentially based upon the idea of sacrifice of life and natural rights, and that both start equally from the same principle; the natural wickedness of man, which according to the church, can be overcome only by Divine Grace, and by the death of the natural man in God, and according to the State, only through law and the immolation of the individual on the altar of the State. Both aim to transform man—one, into a saint, the other, into a citizen. But the natural man has to die, for his condemnation is unanimously decreed by the religion of the church and that of the State.[22]

Atheism and anarchism were therefore closely linked by Bakunin, probably more so than by other anarchist thinkers apart from Proudhon and Stirner, but then Bakunin's anarchism had a socialist dimension quite different from these two more individualist anarchists. Eugène Pyziur has suggested that one of the main reasons for Bakunin's atheism was the close relation evident in Russia between the Russia orthodox church and the Tsarist autocracy.[23] And certainly Bakunin highlighted the way in which religion bolstered political despotism. The equation between the church and the State he admits is an "abstraction" but it is based on real historical facts—violence, conquest, enslavement and the brutal repression of real people. He notes how under feudalism, the power of the aristocratic nobility rested "upon two irrefutable arguments based upon violence, upon brutal physical force and its consecration by God's will . . . the Church bestowed its benediction upon this violence."[24] The "first" and the "divine sanction" were the basis of aristocratic power. The bourgeoisie, on the other hand, sought its sanctions outside of God and Church, and here the theories of popular sovereignty and the "general will" came into play. This is where patriotism comes in as the "transcendent morality" of the State. Patriotism, complements the bourgeoisie's other divine conception—the sacred property.

Bakunin distinguished between natural patriotism, the "passion for solidarity" that not only finds its expression in the animal world, but is found in all human societies. This patriotism is "the instinctive attachment of individuals to all material, intellectual and moral habits which constitute the traditional and customary life of a particular society"[25] which may imply a negative attitude or even hostility towards alien communities. Such customs and habits are second nature to humankind, and Bakunin suggests that need to "humanize society," to create the social conditions which will engender habits and traditions that are conducive to liberty and human well-being. Such natural patriotism expresses a purely natural feeling; it is "the product of the life of a social group united by bonds of genuine solidarity and not yet enfeebled by reflection of the effect of economic and political interests." Such patriotism can only embrace a very restricted world—a tribe, commune or village.[26] But the patriotism advocated by the republican bourgeoisie is quite different—"it is precisely the group interests of this privileged class." Bakunin writes:

> Bourgeois patriotism, as I view it, is only a very shabby, very narrow, especially mercenary and deeply anti-

human passion, having for its object the preservation and maintenance of the power of the national State— that is, the mainstay of all the privileges of the exploiters throughout the nation.[27]

Bourgeois consciousness therefore combines an advocacy of the State and patriotism—which is a negation of human solidarity and equality—with a fanatical worship of property. Natural patriotism, on the other hand, is a "purely local feeling" and a serious obstacle to the formation of States.[28]

NOTES

1. Maximoff, G. P. 1953. ed., *The Political Philosophy of Bakunin: Scientific Anarchism*, Glencoe: Free Press, p. 263.
2. Lehning, A. 1973. *Michael Bakunin: Selected Writings*. London: Cape, pp. 151-52.
3. Maximoff, op. cit., p. 208.
4. Maximoff, op. cit., p. 208.
5. Lehning, op. cit., p. 208.
6. Lehning, op. cit., pp. 204-5.
7. Maximoff, op. cit., pp. 206-8.
8. Lehning, op. cit., p. 264.
9. Maximoff, op. cit., p. 209.
10. Maximoff, op. cit., p. 206.
11. Maximoff, op. cit., p. 208.
12. Maximoff, op. cit., p. 210.
13. Maximoff, op. cit., pp. 211-23.
14. Maximoff, op. cit., pp. 209-213.
15. Maximoff, op. cit., p. 214.
16. Maximoff, op. cit., p. 240.
17. Maximoff, op. cit., pp. 256-58.
18. Maximoff, op. cit., pp. 221-22.
19. Maximoff, op. cit., p. 232.
20. Maximoff, op. cit., p. 224.
21. Maximoff, op. cit., p. 221.
22. Maximoff, op. cit., p. 206.
23. Pyziur, E. 1955. *The Doctrine of Anarchism of Michael Bakunin*, Milwaukee: Regnery, p. 52.
24. Maximoff, op. cit., p. 241.
25. Maximoff, op. cit., p. 229.
26. Maximoff, op. cit., p. 231.
27. Maximoff, op. cit., pp. 232-33.
28. Maximoff, op. cit., pp. 232-33.

Chapter 12

Socialism and Federalism

"**P**HANTOMS**,**" wrote Bakunin, "should not rule and oppress the world which belongs only to living persons"[1]—and the "phantoms" and "abstractions" he had in mind were "God" and the "State." But Bakunin, however, was not only an atheist and a radical liberal critic of the State, but also a socialist, and a critique of capitalism is an important aspect of all his later writings. It is a critique entirely overlooked by his liberal critics like Berlin and Kelly.

Bakunin stressed the intrinsic connection between economic exploitation and political domination. Exploitation is the flesh, domination the soul, he wrote, of the bourgeois State. And like the connection between God and the State, Bakunin almost equates government and exploitation: "to exploit and to govern mean the same thing," he wrote, "one completing the other and in the long run serving as it means and end." But it is clear that he sees domination and exploitation as having a close, dialectical relationship to one another, rather than equating them. As he put it:

> Exploitation and Government are two inseparable expressions of that which is called politics, the first furnishing the means with which the process of governing is carried on, and also constituting the necessary base as well as the goal of all government which in turn guarantees and legalizes the power to exploit.[2]

No one has expressed this relationship so succinctly or in better terms. In the past, this intimate bond between exploitation and government was disguised by religious fictions, he wrote, but the bourgeoisie has since "torn off these rather transparent veils."

In his critique of capitalism and in advocating socialism, Bakunin has been seen as presenting essentially the Marxist position.[3] This is true in a sense. Bakunin always acknowledged his debt to Marx. Bakunin described *Das Kapital* as a "magnificent work" and although he sometimes chaffed at Marx's Hegelian jargon, he nevertheless thought Marx's economic scholarship both "serious and profound."[4]

But in accepting the validity of some of Marx's economic theories this doesn't make Bakunin a Marxist. What it reflects is a lamentable tendency to equate Marxism with socialism, and to accept the ideological hegemony of Marx's own brand of socialism. But in point of fact there were many different styles of socialism in the nineteenth century—insurrectionary (Blanqui), reformist (Blanc, Lasalle), petty-bourgeois (Proudhon), utopian (Fourier) as well as the "scientific socialism" of Marx, and Bakunin's own libertarian socialism. And a critique of capitalist exploitation was by no means unique to Marx.

Bakunin explicitly accepted the socialist critique of laissez-faire capitalism. He wrote:

> Is it necessary to repeat here the irrefutable arguments of socialism, which no bourgeois economist has yet succeeded in disproving? What is property, what is capital in their present form? For the capitalist and the property owner they mean the power and right, guaranteed by the State, to live without working. And since neither property nor capital produces anything when not fertilized by labour—that means the power and the right to live by exploiting the work of someone else. The right to exploit the work of those who possess neither property nor capital and who thus are forced to sell their productive power.[5]

Bakunin tended to agree with Marx and other socialists that "the subordination of labour to capital is the source of all slavery: political, moral and material." Underlying all historical problems—natural, religious, political—there has, he wrote, "always been the economic problem . . . Wealth has always been and still is the indispensable condition for the realization of everything human: authority, power, intelligence, knowledge, freedom."[6] Bakunin consistently advocated a materialist approach to social issues, although this did not imply, any more than it did for Marx, a technological determinism, or a tendency to see culture and consciousness as simply a "reflection" of economic factors. Bakunin was a dialectical or historical materialist, not a mechanical one. But in contemporary society, where the privileged classes, those possessing land, capital and education, exploit the working class, Bakunin believed that a truly human and free society could only be attained through the radical transformation of this system of inequality.

Class struggle was inevitable as long as capitalism existed, for this was a system based on oppression and forced labour. Although the capitalist and worker may be juridical equals, the market nexus, Bakunin argued, was not an equal transaction, but involved the hidden exploitation of the worker. "What happens in the market is a meeting between a drive for lucre and starvation, between master and slave . . . What the economists call equalized supply and demand does not constitute real equality between those who offer their labour for sale and those who purchase it."[7] The worker under capitalism is seen by Bakunin as having the status of a serf, in being forced to sell his or her labour to avoid starvation. Bakunin accepted Lassale's analysis that under capitalism, conditions for the proletariat were becoming increasingly worse each year, and that competition was leading to a growing concentration of wealth, the large industrial enterprises and mercantile firms destroying or absorbing their smaller competitors. The petit-bourgeoisie too, were being increasingly driven into the ranks of the proletariat. Bakunin thus concluded that "so long as property and capital exist on the one hand, and labour on the other, the first constituting the bourgeois class and the other the proletariat, the worker will be the slave and the bourgeois the master."[8] And as we have noted, Bakunin stressed that one of the prime functions of the State was to sustain "the systematic and legalized dominance of the ruling class over the exploited people."[9] Under such conditions, Bakunin asks himself, are fraternity and equality possible between the exploiter and the exploited, are justice and freedom possible for the exploited? Bakunin's response was a negative one. "Can the emancipation of labour signify any other thing but its deliverance from the yoke of property and capital?"[10]

Bakunin came to advocate socialism, and to support those workers who "guided by their admirable sound sense as well as their instincts, realized that the first condition of their real emancipation, or of their humanization, was a radical change in their economic conditions."[11] Bakunin concluded that under the present economic conditions, no liberty was possible for the majority of people—the workers—and all those who called upon them to win political liberties without touching upon the central issue of socialism, were misleading the people.

In his address to the League of Peace and Freedom in 1867 Bakunin reviewed the various theories of socialism which had emerged after the French revolution. This revolution, for Bakunin, as for Kropotkin, was an important watershed in human history. It heralded the first appearance of ordinary people in "politics" and the advent of a new gospel, that of the "rights of man." It proclaimed that all men were equal, and entitled, as humans, to liberty and equality, and that every person should be empowered and given the material and moral means necessary to develop all of their human potential. Babeuf, Bakunin writes, was the last and most pure-hearted of the revolutionaries, and the French revolution culminated with Babouvism. For Babeuf "sought to save the spirit of this revolution by conceiving a political and social system according to which the republic, the expression of the collective will of the citizens, would confiscate all individual property and administer it in the interest of all."[12] The ideal of a socialist republic was developed by Buonarroti, Cabet and Louis Blanc between 1830 and 1848, and a definitive theory of revolutionary socialism was established. Another socialist tradition, which Bakunin described as doctrinaire, was created by Saint-Simon and Fourier, and this was an important tradition in presenting a critique of capitalism that was both profound and scientific. What Fourier and Saint-Simon did not understand is that "while we might enunciate the great principles of humanity's future development, we should leave it to the experience of the future to work out the practical realization of such principles."[13]

But Bakunin's criticism of the early socialists was not only in terms of their "utopianism," he was also critical of their latent authoritarianism. He wrote:

> In general, regulation was the common passion of all the socialists of the pre-1848 era, with one exception only. Cabet, Louis Blanc, the Flourierists, the Saint-Simonists, all were inspired by a passion for indoctrinating and organizing the future; they all were more or less authoritarians. The exception is Proudhon.[14]

As an anarchist who opposed all forms of authority, including State socialism, as an atheist who was also a profound critic of capitalism, Proudhon, Bakunin felt, was instinctively a hundred times more revolutionary than all the doctrinaire and bourgeois socialists. Proudhon's "own socialism was based upon liberty, both individual and collective, and on the spontaneous action of free associations obeying no laws other than the general laws of social economy, already known and yet to be discovered by social science, free from all governmental regulation and State protection. This socialism subordinated politics to the economic, intellectual and moral interests of society. It subsequently, by its own logic, culminated in federalism."[15]

Towards the other "offspring" of the French revolution—republicanism—Bakunin was consistently hostile. He thought it invariably led, as we have earlier noted, to despotism. Bakunin goes on to suggest that what succumbed during the revolutions of 1848 and its aftermath was not socialism in general, but State socialism—the kind of "authoritarian and regimented socialism . . . that had believed and hoped that the State would fully satisfy the needs and legitimate aspirations of the working classes."[16] This form of socialism, in both its reformist (Lasalle) and Marxist variants, Bakunin was to criticize continually during the last decade of his life. He was critical too of the notion that political change (democratic rule) must precede economic change (socialism), believing that this would only further consolidate bourgeois rule.

All complex societies, past and present, Bakunin suggested, rested upon the following foundations: "upon the historic fact of violence, upon the right to inherit property, upon the family rights of the father and the husband, and the consecration of all these foundations by religion. And all that taken together constitutes the essence of the State."[17]

Bakunin placed an important emphasis of the right of inheritance, seeing it as one of the foundations of the capitalist system, and as "begetting" all economic, political and social privileges. "So long as the right of inheritance is in force, there can be no economic, social or political equality in the world."[18] Bakunin therefore always stressed that the emancipation of the working class necessarily implied that the right to inheritance should be abolished and, as we noted earlier, his political programmes to the International Fraternity (1866) and to the League of Peace and Freedom (1867) advocated this. As the latter document put it: The right of inheritance "must necessarily be abolished, we believe, for as long as inheritance is in effect, there will be hereditary economic inequality, not the natural equality of individuals but the artificial inequality of classes."[19] Marx, of course, was to stress that the inheritance laws were an effect, rather than the cause, of class structure.

Yet it was not only in terms of its social and economic equalities that Bakunin criticized the capitalist system; he also criticized it for its excessive, brutalizing character, because "it leaves no room for leisure and deprives men of the possibility of enjoying life in a humane way." Work was neither an evil nor a harsh necessity; it was a vital need for every person, and the day in which the work of body and mind is regarded in its full sense, as a sign of a person's humanity, then "society will be saved."[20]

Divine morality, Bakunin went on to say, "considers work a
degradation and a punishment" but human morality sees it as the
supreme condition of human happiness and human dignity. He was
therefore concerned to break down the barriers between manual and
intellectual labour, and proposed that "great minds" should also contribute to collective manual labour. This would create a feeling of justice and solidarity among such intellectuals, as well as improving their
physical and spiritual strength, and it would also lead to the elevation
and humanization of manual labour.[21] But as Bakunin wrote, there is
work and work, and morality as the bourgeois understands it, consists
of exploiting someone else's labour.[22]

Bakunin's political philosophy involved both an advocacy of liberty and a radical critique of all forms of authority, and a realization that
the capitalist system, with its inherent economic inequalities made such
liberty—in both its negative and positive sense—incapable of being
realized. He was thus both an anarchist and a socialist, an advocate of
both liberty and equality. And he sensed that true human solidarity—
fraternity—was possible only in a society in which both liberty and
equality were safeguarded. He did not, like liberal theorists, see these
as opposing values, as in inherent conflict; to the contrary, he argued
that liberty—real, not abstract (political) liberty—was only possible in
an egalitarian society. Liberty was a sham under capitalism; this he con-
stantly reiterated.

Bakunin expressed this ideal of a libertarian socialist society in the
following declaration to the League of Peace and Freedom:

> As we are convinced that the real attainment of liberty, of
> justice and of peace in the world will be impossible so
> long as the immense majority of the populations are dis-
> possessed of property, deprived of education and con-
> demned to political and social non-being and a *de facto* if
> not a *de jure* slavery, through their state of misery as well
> as their need to labour without rest of leisure, in produc-
> ing all the wealth in which the world is glorying today,
> and receiving in return but a small proportion hardly suf-
> ficient for their daily bread . . .
>
> As we are convinced that liberty without socialism is
> privilege, injustice; and that socialism without liberty is
> slavery and brutality . . .
>
> Now therefore (the League) proclaims the need for a
> radical social and economic reform, whose aim shall be

the deliverance of the people's labour from the yoke of capital and property, upon the foundation of the strictest justice—not juridical, not theological, not metaphysical, but simply human justice, of positive science and the most absolute liberty.[23]

The first condition for the real emancipation of working people therefore, Bakunin contended, rested on a radical change in their economic situation—on the establishment of socialism. Bakunin quotes Aristotle to the effect that in order to think, to feel free and to develop our human potential, a person must be "freed from the preoccupations of the material life."[24] But such a socialist system must be set within the context of liberty. Following Proudhon (who was not in a real sense a socialist for he advocated small-scale property and a market system) Bakunin argued that the only political system in which it was possible to safeguard liberty was a federalist system. This he described in the following terms:

> A truly popular organization begins from below, from the association, from the commune. Thus starting out with the organization of the lowest nucleus and proceeding upward, federalism becomes a political institution of socialism, the free and spontaneous organization of popular life.[25]

In his writings on the Paris Commune he spelt out his ideas on the future society in even clearer terms:

> The abolition of the Church and of the State must be the first and indispensable condition of the real emancipation of society; after which (and only after which) it can, and must, organize itself in a different fashion, but not from the top to bottom, and according to an ideal plan, dreamt up by a few wise men or scholars, or even by a national assembly, elected by universal suffrage. Such a system . . . would lead inevitably to the creation of a new State, and consequently to the formation of a governmental aristocracy . . .
>   The future social organization must be made solely from the bottom upwards, by the free association of federation of workers, firstly in their unions, then in the

communes, regions, nations and finally in a great federation, international and universal. Then only will be realized the true and life-giving order of freedom and the common good, that order which . . . affirms and brings into harmony the interests of individuals and of society.[26]

Bakunin argued that existing States could not form the basis for a true federation, and he stressed that each of the constitutive entities—community, province or nation—must have absolute autonomy. "The right of free reunion, as well as the right of secession, is the first and most important of all political rights; without that right a confederation would simply be a disguised centralization." But for Bakunin this did not imply the social isolation of individual communes or the provinces; indeed he sensed that "unity is the goal towards which humanity irresistibly tends. But it becomes fatal and destructive of the intelligence, dignity, and prosperity of individuals and peoples whenever it is formed by excluding liberty."[27]

Bakunin was not a utopian idealist—whatever his liberal and Marxist critics may say—and he recognized that individuals and communities would have to adapt and conform if they wished to "participate" in wider social units. He allowed a degree of direct democracy. People had the right to be lazy or industrious, but if they chose not to produce or contribute to the common weal then they could not expect to share in the political rights of the community. But Bakunin insists that every person and association is autonomous and has the right not to participate in the wider confederation, and should not be coerced to do so. Rather unfairly, Pyziur argues that Bakunin's libertarian emphasis is simply "verbal incantation" while, in practice, federalism would entail a centralism that would completely outweigh the elements of local autonomy.[28] Such an opinion is a reflection of Pyziur's own political ideas, and is not contained in Bakunin's argument.

It is unclear whether Bakunin advocated a non-market form of socialism. Alain Pengam suggests that Bakunin, like Malatesta, was essentially a left-wing Proudhonist "for whom the abolition of exchange value would have been an aberration."[29] But Bakunin was no advocate of private property, and his socialism is fundamentally "collectivist." As he wrote:

The land belongs only to those who cultivate it with their own hands; to the agricultural communes. The capital and all the tools of production belong to the workers: to the workers' associations . . . The future political organization should be a free federation of workers.[30]

But the nature of the economic ties between these associations and the agricultural or town communes Bakunin never specifies. Pyziur is essentially correct in suggesting that Bakunin gave few hints as to the question of production in a future anarchist society, and raised few questions about distribution and exchange, though Bakunin's writings did imply an end to the wage system. Pyziur's other suggestion that Bakunin only dealt with economic problems to the extent that they made necessary the achievement of his moral and political aims also has a ring of truth about it.

Bakunin clearly saw economic equality as the necessary foundation for liberty and justice, which were his primary values. Nevertheless, socialism—equality—was a central and not a secondary aspect of Bakunin's political philosophy. But Pyziur's stress on Bakunin's moral goals—the realization of the ideals of freedom and equality—makes nonsense of his later contention that Bakunin was an "immoralist" and that his "humanism" was of dubious value.[31] He also stresses Bakunin's violent tactics. Pyziur admits that Bakunin's sociology was in reality a branch of ethics, in that Bakunin argued that social life must be arranged in accordance with moral principles, which are the emanation of reason and conscience.[32] As G. D. H. Cole has stressed, Bakunin was far from being an "immoralist," a label that Bakunin unfairly received from his association with Nechaev. In fact, in most of Bakunin's writings there is no tendency at all towards nihilism—quite the opposite. Bakunin's socialism is highly moralistic, based as it is on certain fundamental moral values—liberty, equality, solidarity, justice, sociality. Bakunin can't win: while some liberals accuse him of living in a fantasy land, playing around with abstract ethical categories that have no connection with reality, other liberals accuse him of being a nihilist and "immoralist." Bakunin was a moralist, but he sought to give human values concrete expression, by examining the reality of existing society, in particular the nature of the State and capitalism, and offered rational arguments for an alternative society—libertarian socialism.

As we shall observe, Bakunin's continual stress on "destruction" has to be interpreted within the context of his social theory. Bakunin was fundamentally a social thinker, and he is concerned, Hegelian fashion, with the negation of human institutions that he saw as oppressive and detrimental to human freedom: he is not an advocate of violence against humans.

A final word may be made in this section regarding Bakunin's attitude to power and authority, both of which he appears to reject in a radical fashion. All human beings possess a natural instinct for power, which Bakunin felt had its origins in the basic law of life enjoining every person to struggle in order to ensure their existence. Thus, everyone carries within themselves the germs of an "cursed element," the lust for power. Bakunin therefore considered it very natural that, in specific social circumstances, when people were put in positions of power, they should take advantage of it and become corrupt. No one is immune from this. Even sincere socialists or revolutionaries, if endowed with positions of power, are apt to make full use of the opportunities offered, whether through vanity, ambition or greed. Bakunin thus concluded that:

> No one should be entrusted with power, inasmuch as anyone invested with authority must, through the force of an immutable social law, become an oppressor and exploiter of society.[33]

But Bakunin does not have a Hobbesian conception of human nature, which regards human subjects as essentially egoistic, aggressive and competitive; on the contrary, he views the human individual as having an innate sense of justice and as being fundamentally social. Individuals are powerfully influenced by their social environment, and for this reason, Bakunin writes, "we demand not natural but social equality of individuals as the condition for justice and the foundations of morality."[34]

Bakunin places a fundamental stress as mentioned, on liberty and the need to abolish all forms of authority, whether human or divine. He emphasizes the need for a form of society that will counter egoism and power-seeking, and will help the "people towards self-determination on the lines of the most complete equality and the fullest freedom in every direction, without the least interferences from any sort of domination."[35] The question is raised and Bakunin himself poses it, whether his critique implies the rejection of all authority. He writes:

> Does it follow that I reject all authority? Perish the thought. In the matter of boots, I defer to the authority of the bootmaker; concerning houses, canals and railroads, I consult the architect or the engineer. For such special knowledge I apply to such a "savant." But I allow neither

the bootmaker nor the architect nor the "savant" to impose his authority on me . . . If I bow before the authority of the specialists, willing to accept their suggestions and their guidance for a time and to a degree, I do so only because I am not compelled to by anyone . . . I bow before the authority of specialists because it is imposed upon me by my own reason.[36]

Although Bakunin writes with passion and conviction and often uses terms that imply "absolutes," in point of fact, Bakunin did not think in terms of absolutes at all—although he certainly saw liberty and justice as supreme values that ought to be realized concretely in human society. Pyziur's suggestions that Bakunin anarchism was simply an "amalgam" of collectivism and individualism, though Bakunin was "never able to formulate their relationship,"[37] is simply untrue. Bakunin's anarchism was itself a concrete outline and synthesis of these two doctrines, for he saw—as Pyziur admits—the ideals of liberty (individualism) and equality (collectivism or socialism) as mutually interdependent. As Bakunin so succinctly put it: "Freedom without socialism is injustice, socialism without freedom is brutality." Liberals, as apologists for capitalism, represent bourgeois individualism; Marxists represent the second position—that of State socialism. Bakunin's anarchism was a sustained and reasoned attempt to unite, in a dialectical synthesis, liberalism (the stress on liberty and individualism) with socialism (the stress on equality as a necessary condition for concrete liberty). As Pyziur writes, the two ideals—liberty and equality—"were brought into reciprocal interdependence and though not considered interchangeable, they were regarded as two facets of the highest value, justice."[38] Bakunin, of course, was as much a historical sociologist as a moralist, and he not only offered a critique of existing institutions, but outlined, however briefly, the nature of a society in which this "synthesis" would be correctly embodied. Pyziur's response to Bakunin's vision is to suggest that "both common sense and historical experience teach us that liberty, in the sense of a wide choice for each individual in determining his way of life, is incompatible with a rigidly egalitarian society."[39] Common sense and history teach us nothing of the kind. On the contrary, the realities of capitalism and the modern State suggest that Bakunin's "prophetic mania" offer us a reasoned vision of a future socialist society where liberty is not a sham.

NOTES

1. Maximoff, G. P., ed., 1953. *The Political Philosophy of Bakunin: Scientific Anarchism.* Glencoe: Free Press, p. 245.
2. Maximoff, op. cit., p. 132.
3. Pyziur, E. 1955. *The Doctrine of Anarchism of Michael Bakunin,* Milwaukee: Regnery, p. 55.
4. Lehning, A. 1973. *Michael Bakunin: Selected Writings.* London: Cape, p. 244.
5. Maximoff, op. cit., p. 180.
6. Maximoff, op. cit., p. 358.
7. Maximoff, op. cit., pp. 185-6.
8. Maximoff, op. cit., p. 181.
9. Maximoff, op. cit., p. 365.?????
10. Maximoff, op. cit., p. 181.?????
11. Maximoff, op. cit., p. 192.
12. Dolgoff, S. 1973. ed., trans, introd., *Bakunin on Anarchy,* New York: Knopf, p. 115.
13. Dolgoff, op. cit., p. 116.
14. Dolgoff, op. cit., p. 116
15. Dolgoff, op. cit., p. 117.
16. Dolgoff, op. cit., p. 121.
17. Maximoff, op. cit., p. 242.
18. Maximoff, op. cit., p. 243.
19. Dolgoff, op. cit., p. 126.
20. Maximoff, op. cit., pp. 244-45.
21. Pyziur, op. cit., pp. 136-7.
22. Maximoff, op. cit., p. 135.
23. Dolgoff, op. cit., p. 128.
24. Maximoff, op. cit., p. 276.
25. Maximoff, op. cit., p. 273-4.
26. Lehning, op. cit., pp. 205-6.
27. Maximoff, op. cit., p. 275.
28. Pyziur, op. cit., p. 133.
29. Pengam, A. 1987. "Anarcho-Communism." In M. Rubel & J. Crump (eds.). *Non-Market Socialism in the 19th and 20th Centuries.* London: MacMillan, p. 67.
30. Maximoff, op. cit., p. 247.
31. Pyziur, op. cit., p. 123.
32. Pyziur, op. cit., p. 117.
33. Maximoff, op. cit., p. 249.
34. Maximoff, op. cit., p. 249.
35. Lehning, op. cit., p. 191.
36. Dolgoff, op. cit., p. 229.
37. Pyziur, op. cit., p. 47.
38. Pyziur, op. cit., p. 121.
39. Pyziur, op. cit., p. 12.

Chapter 13

The Critique of Marxism

W E have in the first part of this study discussed the "great schism" as James Joll (1964) called it, which emerged in the International Working Men's Association in the early 1870s, and which focused around the personal dispute between Marx and Bakunin. But as Cole and others have suggested, this schism was not simply a clash of personalities; it involved two factions within the socialist movement and two quite different conceptions of socialism, of the processes of revolutionary change and the conditions for human liberation. The dispute eventually crystallized towards the end of the century in the development of two separate and distinctive movements—social democracy (Marxism) and anarchism. But the grounds for the dispute were clearly spelled out in Bakunin's own writings, particularly in his study *Statism and Anarchy* (1873), the first completed volume of a larger projected work. And it may be useful to review here the main themes in Bakunin's important critique of Marx—a critique that still has contemporary relevance.

It has often been suggested that Marx and Bakunin were in fundamental agreement as to the aims of the revolutionary movement; both were revolutionaries who sought to consolidate the international solidarity of workers in order to achieve a society that was both socialist and Stateless. Where they differed was in the means for achieving this end. In separating Marx from Lenin and his Bolshevik disciples, Maxmilien Rubel has even suggested that Marx was not an authoritarian socialist but rather the "first to develop a theory of anarchy."[1] But while Marx and Bakunin undoubtedly have certain common aims—a socialist economy, the disappearance of the State as a repressive institution, the end of class rule—the ultimate visions of both men, as John Clark (1984) has explored, are fundamentally distinct. The future envisaged by Marx and Engels looked to a high development of industrial technology with a corresponding degree of centralized institutions through which the economy and social life would be "managed." "Productive" activity was seen as a primary concern in their future communist society. In contrast, the anarchist view, articulated by Bakunin, saw the "human scale" as essential, both in production and in the institutions arising from the new models of association. The emphasis is on cultural interactions and the person's enjoyment of free social activity, rather than on productive concerns. And although Bakunin succumbs at times to revolutionary asceticism, he nevertheless asserts that the socialist "takes his stand on his positive right to life and all its pleasures, both intellectual, moral and physical. He loves life, and intends to enjoy it to the full."[2] Bakunin continually contrasted "life" and the "natural" aspects of human existence with "abstractions" and "artificiality," and it is clear where his own sympathies lay. The human subject he felt was the continuation of the work, creation, movement and life of Nature itself, and no intellectual or institutional forms should hinder the liberty and creativity of the individual. Clark concludes that in spite of the oft-repeated clichés about the two ideals being the same, there were in fact significant differences of emphasis in the visions of Marx and Bakunin.[3]

Bakunin, as we have earlier stressed, adopted a materialist approach to reality, and continually emphasized the priority of the economic aspects of human life. In *God and the State,* he suggested, as we noted, that the whole history of humanity, intellectual and moral, political and social, is "but a reflection of its economic history."[4] Likewise in *The Political Theology of Mazzini,* Bakunin sums up his own materialist outlook as follows:

> Just as in the material world proper, inorganic matter (mechanical, physical, chemical) is the determinant of organic matter (vegetable, animals, mental), so in the social world, which in any case can only be considered as the highest known development of the material world, the development of economic forces has always been and still continues to be the determinant of all religious, philosophical, political and social developments.[5]

Bakunin's world outlook is therefore fundamentally the same as that of Hegel and Marx—evolutionary, dialectical, materialist (Hegel spoke of his own philosophy as objective idealism) and deterministic. In an important critique of Marx's historical materialism, John Clark has suggested[6] that in making a distinction between "the material production of life" and "forms of consciousness," and seeing the former as the "basis" of human history, Marx's overall perspective was to suggest a "productive view of history" which sees consciousness and culture as "having merely a derivative status," and reduced human thought "to a

reflection of material reality." Marx had, Clark writes, "an objective conception of materialism which created a barrier to the achievement of a
fully materialist and fully dialectical view." There has been much debate,
of course, on Marx's philosophy of history and on the degree to which
he can or cannot be considered an economic or technological deter-
minist. The important point however is that the criticisms levelled at
Marx by Clark could equally well have been levelled at Bakunin. But
Clark's critique of Marx (and implicitly of Bakunin's overall perspective), though having a degree of truth in stressing Marx's productivism
and Promethean tendency, is somewhat unfair and one-sided—to both
Marx and Bakunin. Two provisos need to be made.

Firstly, when Marx speaks of the "production of material life" as
"conditioning" and "determining" other aspects of social life, it is clearly misleading to interpret this as implying a simple causal relationship
between the economic "base" and the cultural "superstructure." To do
so invokes a mechanistic paradigm that is quite alien to the thought of
both Marx and Bakunin. As Merleau-Ponty put it, the economic base is
not the "cause" but the "historical anchorage" of law, religion and other
cultural phenomena. The metaphor Marx uses is a spatial one, and the
relationship between "material" conditions and the other aspects of
culture is analogous to the relationship between the earth's substratum
and soil. Stressing the conditioning effects of the economy does not
deny the autonomy of "culture" cited by Clark, which is an idealist
perspective that Bakunin would have rejected, however cogent
Sahlin's critique of sociobiology.

Secondly, it is misleading to conceive of consciousness and culture
as somehow distinct from the economy, for, as Cole long ago suggested,
"ideas" and "mind" are a part of what Marx conceived of as the
"material." The economic base, for Marx as for Bakunin, was those important social relations that humans had been obliged to establish
among themselves in the production of their material life. Bakunin was
a "productivist" only in the sense that he saw human interaction with
nature as a creative activity that formed the "basis" of the other aspects
of social life—moral, religious, philosophical. He specifically criticized
the idea that humans were separate from nature. Those anthro-
pologists who stress the uniqueness and autonomy of culture and the
symbolic order are much closer in fact philosophically to the perspectives of Descartes and mechanistic philosophy than are the "produc-
tivists" Marx and Bakunin.

Nevertheless, Clark's analysis is essentially correct in indicating
that Marx continually emphasized the determining effects of the

economy, and down-played the autonomy and importance of individuals as creative beings and of other aspects of social life. And it
was this productivism and rigid economic determinism that Bakunin
himself found unacceptable. In challenging Marx's notion that only industrial workers in advanced industrial nations like Germany, Britain
and France could be truly revolutionary—given his economic theory—
Bakunin wrote that Marx seemed unable to acknowledge the liberty of
workers in other countries. Bakunin continues:

> The political State in every country, he says, is always the
> product and faithful reflection of its economic situation;
> to change the former, one has only to change the latter.
> This is the whole secret of political evolutions, according
> to Marx. He pays no heed to other elements in history,
> such as the effect—obvious though it is—of political,
> judicial and religious institutions on the economic situa-
> tion. He says that "hardship produces political slavery—
> the State," but does not allow for the converse: Political
> slavery—the State—reproduces and maintains hardship
> as a condition of its existence . . . Marx also utterly ignores
> one highly important element in the historical develop-
> ment of humanity, and that is the individual tempera-
> ment and character of all races and people, which are
> themselves a product of a host of ethnographic,
> climatological and economic, as well as historical causes,
> but which, once established, exert considerable influence
> over the economic forces.[7]

Bakunin stresses the autonomy and determining influences of cultural factors, allowing for a greater potential for human liberation than
Marx was willing to admit. This did not imply a rejection of his
materialism, only the limitation of monocausal explanations that Marx
was prone to adopt. But Bakunin also stresses another element that
needed to be taken into account—the instinct of rebellion—whose influence on history was, he suggested, "primordial." As against Marx's
economic determinism, Bakunin left more room for the human will, but
as we shall see, this did not imply that he was a "voluntarist" and
thought that a revolution would happen overnight. But Bakunin did
tend to overstress the "national character" of respective peoples, er-
roneously believing that Latin and Slavic people were somehow more
"libertarian by nature."[8]

A second major difference between Bakunin and Marx lay in their contrasting conceptions of the revolutionary transition, for Marx, as with other authoritarian socialists, saw the transition as involving the "conquest of political power by the proletariat," the seizure of State power by the workers. As Marx and Engels expressed it in the famous "Manifesto of the Communist Party" (1848):

> The first step in the revolution . . . is to raise the proletariat to the position of the ruling class, to win the battle for democracy.
>
> The proletariat will use its political supremacy to wrest, by degrees, all capital from the bourgeoisie, to centralize all instruments of production in the hands of the State, i.e. of the proletariat organized as the ruling class.

The communist party is seen as representing the proletarian movement in its "violent overthrow of the bourgeoisie."[9]

Marxists have long debated just exactly what this entailed, and whether or not the Bolshevik take-over of State power in Russia in 1917 exemplified what Marx himself had envisaged. But the important point is that Bakunin consistently repudiated and criticized this whole conception of revolution. For Bakunin, only libertarian means could be used to create a libertarian socialist society; recourse to State power, whether or not this allowed parliamentary democracy or Blanquist insurrectionary methods, inevitably led to despotism and an end to the revolution. Liberty, as he put it, "can only be created by liberty, that is by mass rebellion and the free organization of the working masses from the bottom upwards."[10]

This different conception of revolution, and his hostility towards the strategy of the State socialists, came to the fore in the struggles within the International during the years 1871-1873. It was then that Bakunin outlined his critique of Marx and his own thoughts on a Stateless social order. This is to be found in his two studies—*The Knouto-Germanic Empire and the Social Revolution* (1871-72) and *Statism and Anarchy* (1873)—as well as in a long letter to *La Liberté*, dated October 5, 1872, which he never sent or completed. The essence of his disagreement with Marx was clearly articulated immediately after the Paris Commune, for in his writings on the insurrection Bakunin made a clear distinction between the revolutionary collectivists and the "authoritarian communists who support the absolute power of the

State." Although their ultimate aim, he suggests, is identical, they differ in tactics.

> The communists believe it necessary to organize the
> workers' forces to seize the political power of the State.
> The revolutionary socialists organize for the purpose of
> destroying—or, to put it more politely—liquidating the
> State. The communists advocate the principle and the
> practices of authority; the revolutionary socialists put all
> their faith in liberty . . . The revolutionary socialists hold
> that there is a great deal more practical good sense and
> wisdom in the instinctive aspirations and real need of the
> masses than in the profound intelligence of all the doc-
> tors and guides of humanity.[11]

Marx, along with Engels, Lasalle and members of the Social
Democratic Party in Germany all followed, Bakunin contended, the
authoritarian communist (or State socialist) tendency. The split in the
International represented fundamentally different conceptions of
socialism, as even Marx and Engels in their continual jibes and
criticisms of Bakunin accepted—leaving aside the acrimony of some of
their unfounded accusations. In his letter to *La Liberté*, Bakunin unam-
biguously outlined the issue that so deeply divided him from Marx and
his followers:

> We do not see how it is possible to talk about internation-
> al solidarity and yet to intend preserving States—unless
> in some dream of the universal State, meaning universal
> slavery, the dream of the great emperors and popes—be-
> cause by its very nature the State is a branch of that
> solidarity and therefore a permanent cause of war. Nor
> can we conceive how it is possible to talk about the liber-
> ty of the masses within and by means of the State. State
> means dominion, and the dominion involves the sub-
> jugation of the masses and, consequently, their exploita-
> tion for the sake of some ruling minority.
> We do not accept, even in the process of revolution-
> ary transition, either constituent assemblies, pro-
> visional governments or so-called revolutionary dicta-
> torships; because we are convinced that revolution is
> only sincere, honest and real in the hands of the mas-

ses, and that when it is concentrated into those of a few ruling individuals it inevitably and immediately becomes reaction . . .

The Marxists express quite different ideas. They are worshippers of State power, and necessarily also prophets of political and social discipline and champions of order established from the top downwards, always in the name of universal suffrage and the sovereignty of the masses . . . the only kind of emancipation the Marxists accept is what they expect to come out of their so-called People's State (Volkstaat).[12]

These two attitudes, Bakunin concluded, split the International into two camps, and between the libertarian socialists and the Marxists there was indeed an "abyss." Bakunin could not understand how Marx could fail to see that a revolutionary dictatorship would inevitably "kill revolution and warp and paralyse all popular movements."[13] But Bakunin was also critical of Marx's emphasis on the proletariat as the only revolutionary class.

There is another expression in that programme (of the German Social Democratic Party) which is deeply antipathetic to us revolutionary anarchists who unconditionally advocate full popular emancipation and that is the designation of the proletariat, the world of workers, as class rather than as mass. Do you know what this means? Nothing more or less than a new aristocracy, that of the urban and industrial workers, to the exclusion of the millions who make up the rural proletariat and who, in the provisions of the German social democratic, will in effect become subjects of this great so-called popular State.[14]

Bakunin is critical of many different aspects of the programme Marx and Engels outlined in the "Communist Manifesto," and which was essentially incorporated into the programme of the German Social Democratic party founded in 1869, under the auspices of Marx, by Liebknecht and Bebel. He was critical of its stress on the proletariat as the only revolutionary class, of its advocacy of a People's State based on universal suffrage, on its tendency to suggest that crucial aspects of life would be organized through the State, implying the formation of a system of State capitalism rather than socialism; Bakunin had the feeling that such a programme would inevitably lead to a new form of class-rule—rule by a technocratic intelligentsia. These various criticisms will be addressed in the next section.

NOTES

1. Rubel, M. 1987. *Non-Market Socialism in the Nineteenth Century.* In M. Rubel & J. Crump (eds.). *Non-Market Socialism in the 19th and 20th Centuries.* London: MacMillan, p. 26.
2. Lehning, A. 1973. *Michael Bakunin: Selected Writings.* London: Cape, p. 101.
3. Clark, J. 1984. *The Anarchist Movement.* Montreal: Black Rose Books, p. 68.
4. Lehning, op. cit., p. 111.
5. Lehning, op. cit., pp. 223-224.
6. Clark, op. cit., pp. 33-64.
7. Lehning, op. cit., p. 256.
8. Dolgoff, S. 1973. ed., trans, introd., *Bakunin on Anarchy,* New York: Knopf, p. 15.
9. Marx, K. & Engels, F. 1968. *Selected Works.* London: Lawrence & Wishort, pp. 45-52.
10. Lehning, op. cit., p. 270.
11. Dolgoff, op. cit., p. 263.
12. Lehning, op. cit., pp. 237-38.
13. Lehning, op. cit., p. 240.
14. Lehning, op. cit., pp. 253-54.

Chapter 14

Marx and the Dictatorship of the Proletariat

MARX contended that the revolution would essentially entail the founding of a workers' State that would involve "the proletariat elevated to the status of the governing class," and he also stressed that the proletariat was the agency of revolutionary change. He continually rebuked Bakunin for suggesting that revolution could be initiated in countries like Russia, Italy and Spain where industrial capitalism had not yet developed. Revolution for Bakunin was not based on "economic prerequisites," Marx argued; he wants, "the revolution, which is based on the economic foundation of capitalist production, to be carried out on the level of the Russian or Slav agricultural or pastoral nations." Thus, Bakunin's idea of a revolution was based on "will," Marx suggests, not on the economic conditions involving the formation and consolidation of a proletariat class.[1]

Bakunin stressed two things. One was that the proletariat was often, in specific circumstances, not all that revolutionary—sometimes forming an aristocracy of labour. There exists in Germany and Switzerland, he wrote, a numerous class of bourgeois workers, "a special category of relatively affluent workers, earning higher wages, boasting of their literary capacities, and so impregnated by a variety of bourgeois prejudices that, excepting income, they differ in no way from the bourgeois."[2] It was this semi-bourgeois "aristocracy of labour" that, he felt, the Marxists wanted to establish as a ruling class over the peasants and other categories of workers—something Marx dismissed as "schoolboy nonsense," without scrutinizing the implications of what Bakunin was trying to convey.

But, more important, Bakunin also stressed the revolutionary potential of peasants, the lumpen-proletariat and other *déclassé* elements. While, unfortunately, many industrial workers, he wrote, were only too deeply saturated with all the political and social prejudices of the bourgeoisie, the lumpen-proletariat constitute the "flower of the proletariat." The millions of uncultured and disinherited workers, who Marx and Engels contemptuously dismiss as the "lumpen-

proletariat"—the "riffraff," the "scum," the "dregs of society"—
Bakunin believed to have revolutionary potential and to carry "in its
inner being and in its aspiration, all the necessities and miseries of its
collective life, all the seeds of the socialism of the future."[3]

Bakunin also stressed the revolutionary potential of the
peasantry—a class that Marx has regarded, given their attachment to
private landed property and their "dispersed" social life, as essentially
reactionary, inevitably on the side of counterrevolution. It is clear from
Bakunin's writings on the Russian peasant that he did not have, as with
the Russian populists, a romantic image of the people, or of the Russian
commune. Kelly's suggestion that Bakunin had little knowledge of the
Russian peasant and an "idealized" conception of the "people"[4] is not
borne out by Bakunin's own writings, which indicate a clear understanding of the realities of Russian peasant life. In *Statism and Anarchy,*
Bakunin weighed the pros and cons regarding the revolutionary
potential of the Russian peasantry. On the negative side, he pointed to
the ignorance and religious superstitions of the peasants and their
devotion to the Tsar, the patriarchy within the peasant family which
also permeated the commune, the social isolation of the peasant communes as "closed" communities, and the "absorption" of the individual
by the *mir.* Against this, he set the more positive aspects, three fundamental traits that characterize the ideal of the Russian peasant.

> The first of these traits is the conviction, held by all the
> people, that the land rightly belongs to them. The second
> trait is the belief that the benefit from the soil belongs not
> to an individual but to the rural community as a whole, to
> the *mir* which assigns the temporary use of the land to
> members of the community. The third trait is that even
> the minimal limitations placed by the State on the *mir's*
> autonomy arouse hostility on the part of the latter toward
> the State.[5]

In his discussion of French peasantry, Bakunin likewise drew atten-
tion to the revolutionary limitations of the peasants—their avarice,
their unbridled egoism, their fanatic commitment to the individual
ownership of land, and their platonic attachments to the emperor. But
who in present society is not a egoist, or not avaricious, holding on
"passionately to the little property they have been able to scrape
together," Bakunin asks. And contrasting the peasants with the urban
workers, he writes:

It is true that the peasants are not communists. They hate
and fear those who would abolish private property . . .
The vast majority of city workers, owning no property,
are immeasurably more inclined towards communism
than are the peasants. Nothing is more natural; the communism of one is just as natural as the individualism of
the other, but this is no reason to praise the workers for
their communist inclinations, nor to reproach the
peasants for their individualism. The ideas and passions
of both are conditioned by their different environments.

There is no point of extolling or denigrating the
peasants. It is a question of establishing a programme of
action which will overcome the individualism and con-
servatism of the peasants and not only prevent their individualism from propelling them into the camp of the
reaction, but enable that individualism to serve and ensure the triumph of revolution.[6]

Bakunin, therefore, unlike Marx, stressed the revolutionary potential of both the lumpen-proletariat and the peasants, and the need to establish revolutionary connections between urban factory workers and
peasants. His overall assessment of revolution was cogently expressed
in *Letters to a Frenchman* (1870). "I believe that right now in France, and
probably in other countries as well, there exists only two classes
capable of such a movement; the workers and the peasants."[7]

The contrast between Marx and Bakunin on the issue of revolutionary agency was succinctly outlined by G. D. H. Cole:

For Marx, the significant aspect of the contemporary class
struggle was the developing consciousness and organization of the industrial workers, and particularly of those
who were subject to the conditions of advanced large-
scale capitalism. Bakunin, on the other hand, thought of
the revolution much more in terms of the instinctive revolt
of the most oppressed and down-trodden groups in
society—the peasants in relatively backward areas and the
lumpen-proletariat of such cities as Naples, in which
modern industrialism had hardly taken root at all.[8]

Bakunin did not deny the revolutionary potential of the
proletariat; he rather sought to broaden the base of the international

revolutionary movement by emphasizing the need for a united front of all exploited workers—urban workers, peasants and the lumpen-proletariat.[9]

History seems to have proved that Bakunin was right. As Paul Avrich writes:

> We can see then why Bakunin, rather than Marx, can claim to be the true prophet of modern revolution. The three greatest revolutions of the twentieth century—in Russia, Spain and China—have all occurred in relatively backward countries and have largely been "peasant wars" linked with outbursts of the urban poor as Bakunin predicted. The peasantry and the unskilled workers, groups for whom Marx expressed disdain, have become the mass base of twentieth-century social upheavals—upheavals which, though often labelled "Marxist" are more accurately described as "Bakuninist." Bakunin's visions, moreover, have anticipated the social ferment within the Third World, the modern counterpart on a global scale of Bakunin's backward, peripheral Europe.[10]

Exactly what the "conquest of political power by the proletariat" or the concept of a "workers' State" implied, Bakunin was never too sure, as these conceptions are both rather vague. He sensed that it implied the rule of the proletariat as a class over other social elements (the peasantry) and the advocacy of universal suffrage, both of which, he argued, in reality meant the rule of some class or elite. In *Statism and Anarchy*, Bakunin explicitly examined the issue regarding the conquest of political (State) power by the proletariat. He writes:

> One may well ask whether the proletariat would be in the position of a ruling class, and over whom would it rule? This means that yet another proletariat would emerge, which would be subject to the new sovereignty and the new State. For instance, the Marxists, as is well known, are not yet well disposed towards the peasant rabble, who, being on the lowest cultural level, would doubtless be governed by the urban and factory proletariat.
> What does raising the proletariat to the level of government mean? Surely, the whole proletariat is not

going to head for administration? There are about forty million Germans. Does it mean that all forty million will be members of the government? Will all the people be rulers, and will there be no one to be ruled? In that case there will be no government and no State.

This dilemma in the Marxist theory can easily be solved. A people's administration, according to them, must mean a people's administration by virtue of a small number of representatives chosen by the people. The universal right of each individual among all the people to elect so-called representatives and members of the government, that is the final word of the Marxists and of the democratic school, and it is a deception which would conceal the despotism of a governing minority, all the more dangerous because it appears as a sham expression of the people's will.[11]

If the new rulers are workers then, Bakunin argues, they will soon cease to be workers: if they are "dedicated" or learned socialists, then the so-called people's State "will be nothing but a despotic control of the populace by a new and not at all numerous aristocracy of real and pseudo-scientists."[12]

There is a flagrant contradiction in Marxist theory, Bakunin suggests:

If their State would be really of the people, why eliminate it? And if the State is needed to emancipate the workers, then the workers are not yet free, so why call it a People's State.[13]

But what Bakunin senses in the practices of the Marxists and in their revolutionary theory, is the emergence of a new form of bureaucratic State control, a new form of despotism under the control of scientific technocrats. The concentration of all capital and instruments of production in the State (argued by Marx) will eventually lead to the patrimony of a bureaucratic class, and to a government of the intelligentsia. "It will be the reign of scientific intelligence, the most aristocratic, despotic, arrogant and elitists of all regimes."[14]

Marx was a socialist democrat whose programme involves an "out-and-out cult of the State." His programme Bakunin writes, "is a complete network of political and economic institutions rigidly centralized and highly authoritarian, sanctioned, no doubt, like all despotic institutions in modern society, by universal suffrage."[15] Bakunin points out that capitalist production inexorably entails the enormous centralization of the State. However:

> Representative government harmonizes marvellously with the capitalist economic system. This new statist system, basing itself on the alleged sovereignty of the so-called will of the people, was supposedly expressed by their alleged representatives in mock popular assemblies, and incorporates the two principal and necessary conditions for the progress of capitalism: State centralization and the actual submission of the sovereign people to the intellectual governing minority, who, while claiming to represent the people, unfailingly exploits them.[16]

The modern State is based essentially on military and bureaucratic centralization, and the "people's State" of the Marxists involves in essence an administrative machine that rules the masses from above, through a privileged elite of intellectuals, who imagine they know what the people need and want, better than do the people themselves.[17]

Bakunin essentially interprets Marxism "scientific socialism"—as a variant of State communism that implies the rule of an intellectual or bureaucratic elite, whether in the transition period this is regarded as a revolutionary dictatorship or eventually as a ruling intelligentsia. And, he concludes that "the organization and the rule of the new society by socialist savants is the worst of all despotic governments."[18]

Bakunin was by no means an anti-rationalist, for he had a firm belief in the value of positive science, particularly to counter the abstractions of theology and idealist metaphysics. Science, he suggested, was concerned to posit generalizations that express the nature and logic of things, their relations and the laws of their development. After the revolution, science will probably remain a specialist activity, though it will cease to be accessible only to a very few of the privileged class. It ought to be made the "patrimony" of as many people as possible. Science, Bakunin felt, was indispensable to the rational organizations of society but being incapable of dealing with that which is real and living, or with the individuality of the human subject, "it must not interfere with the real or practical organization of society." The sole mission of science is to "light" the way; only life itself, free from all governmental control and given the liberty of spontaneous action is capable of creation. What I preach then, Bakunin wrote, is "up to a certain point, the revolt of life against science, or rather against government by science, not the destruction of science, for that would be a high crime against humanity—but the putting of science in its rightful place."[19]

Elsewhere he wrote;

> It would be sad for mankind if at any time theoretical speculation became the only source of guidance for society, if science alone were in charge of all social administration. Life would wither, and human society would turn into a voiceless and servile herd. The domination of life by science can have no other result than the brutalization of mankind.[20]

Hal Draper's suggestion[21] that Bakunin was a theoretician who was concerned to preach "anti-intellectualism" for the masses, while keeping theory and "dictatorial domination" in the hands of himself and his "band of lumpen-intellectuals" represents a complete falsification of Bakunin's ideas and intentions.

A final difference between Bakunin and Marx relates to the issue of nationalism, which Bakunin felt Marx tended to dismiss as having any relevance to revolutionary struggles. Bakunin's views on this are complex and ambivalent, for his political career essentially involved his development from being a revolutionary nationalist to that of a mature anarchist. At the end of his days he was completely opposed to any form of pan-Slavism, although he still held stereotypic views on the national character of various people, believing the Germans to be inherently rational, hardworking and learned, but lacking in the love of liberty and in the instinct of rebellion, while the Slavs he viewed as essentially freedom-loving people. But the experiences of the 1860s and his dispute with Mazzini made Bakunin realize that many nationalist movements had reactionary implications. As Caroline Cahm writes, Bakunin came to make "explicit what was implicit in his 'Appeal to the Slavs'," namely, that nationality has to be seen in the context of the supreme principle of liberty; it could not in itself be elevated into a principle because it separated peoples and could be associated with a threat to liberty."[22] Nationality, Bakunin wrote, was not a humanitarian principle, "it is a historical, local fact which should be generally tolerated along with other real and inoffensive facts."[23] All people—ethnic groups—have their own specific character, style of life, speech and way of thinking, and it is precisely this style of life that constitutes its nationality. Every people, like every individual, have an incontestable right to be themselves. But this right or nationality should not be regarded as an absolute, exclusive principle. On the contrary, Bakunin writes, the less preoccupied people are with themselves and the "more they are imbued by the general idea of humanity, the more life-giving, the more purposeful, and the more profound becomes the feeling of nationality and individuality."[24] Thus, Bakunin condemned the kind of nationality advocated by aggressive States and nationalist movements like those of Mazzini, who renounced socialism and advocated statist principles. Bakunin, Cahm concluded, unlike Marx and other revolutionaries, "appreciated the importance of national loyalties and aspirations in the context of social revolution. Where other revolutionary socialists dismissed this as a creation of the ruling classes rather than as a strong, natural and instinctive feeling."[25]

Bakunin's critique of Marxism and of the dominion of life by science and technocratic imperatives, has been seen by many writers as profound and as having a contemporary salience.

In an age where managerial and bureaucratic techniques are ubiquitous, where corporate capitalism and State bureaucracies are closely enmeshed and given ideological support by a representative government system based on universal suffrage, where the scientific "establishment" is geared largely to serving State and capitalist interests and is centrally concerned with research into weapons of mass destruction, Bakunin's writings have been described as prescient. Anyone who reads the writings of Marx and Engels on the State and the economy must inevitably conclude that they are permeated by a logic of productivism, and imply an attachment to centralist and authoritarian structures that are inseparable from statist and bureaucratic forms of domination. Bakunin's fears that under Marx's kind of socialism the workers would continue to labour under a regimented, mechanized, hierarchical system of production, without direct control over the product of their labour, has been more than confirmed by the realities of the Bolshevik system. Thus, Bakunin's critique of Marxism has taken on an increasing relevance in the age of bureaucratic State capitalism.[26]

Marxists have generally been dismissive or have simply not engaged themselves with Bakunin's critique of Marx. It has been argued that the General Council of the International never had authoritarian tendencies, that Marx never advocated rule by "socialist savants" and that Bakunin mischievously equated Lasalle's notion of the "people's State" with Marx's quite different conception of the "conquest of political power by the proletariat." It has also been stressed that the idea that Marx opposed the peasants is something of a myth. In concluding this section it is perhaps worthwhile to briefly examine these points.

Firstly, Marx's attitude to the peasants, whom he condemned to the "idiocy of rural life." Marx never in fact considered the peasantry suitable as a revolutionary vanguard—this is patent; what he did argue was that the proletariat should do everything to "win over" the peasants to the revolution. It is also evident that Marx was fundamentally concerned with the "nationalization of land," with the maintenance of large estates and was opposed not only to private property, but also to any communal property on a local basis. In Marx's scheme of things peasants were allowed little autonomy.

Secondly, what did Marx's concept of the "conquest of political power by the proletariat" or the "dictatorship of the proletariat" imply? Was Bakunin correct in maintaining that it implied statist principles? Marx seems to have used the latter terms at two principal periods in his career: in the aftermath of the 1848 revolution and at the time of the Paris Commune. Its meaning has been spelled out by Hal Draper whose sympathy for Bakunin and whose understanding of anarchism approaches zero. Draper writes:

> For Marx and Engels, from beginning to end of their careers and without exception "dictatorship of the proletariat" meant nothing more and nothing less than "rule of the proletariat"—the "conquest of political power" by the working class, the establishment of a workers' State in the immediate post-revolutionary period.[27]

But what does the establishment of a workers' State entail? To answer this it is worth looking at Marx and Engel's address to the Central Committee of the Communist League (March 1850). This is what they essentially argue:

- that the workers must keep themselves independent of the radical bourgeoisie and work for the creation of an independent workers' party, both secret and open.
- that alongside the official liberal government, the workers must simultaneously establish their own revolutionary workers' governments, either in the form of local executive committees and councils or through workers' clubs.

- that the proletariat must arm themselves and organize themselves independently as a proletariat guard.
- that workers should aim "for one German republic but also, within this republic, for the most decisive centralization of power in the hands of the State authority." Under no circumstances can the local autonomy of any village, town or province be tolerated.
- that workers, through the democratic government, should force "the concentration of as many productive forces as possible— means of transport, factories, railways etc—in the hands of the State."[28]

These extracts make it clear that Marx's idea of a workers' State envisaged a democratic republic with a high degree of centralized administration, and that the revolutionary process would involve the setting up of a "counter-State power," not to eliminate the bourgeois State, but rather to replace it. This seemed to be what happened in Russia in 1917—leading to the repressive Bolshevik State. Bakunin's critique of Marx then, was not just part of a smear campaign against Marx, but contained some important criticisms of Marx's whole revolutionary strategy. For Bakunin realized—feared—that any State structure, whether or not socialist or based on universal suffrage, has a certain independence from the society, and so may serve the interests of those within State institutions rather than the people as a whole or the proletariat. Alan Carter suggests that Marx's theory of history, which tended to reduce political power to economic interests, precluded any concern on the part of Marx, with the potentially authoritarian and oppressive outcome of centralized revolutionary methods.[29]

Without any serious discussion of Marx's theory of revolution or of Bakunin's substantive response to it, Aileen Kelly concludes:

> The elaborate edifice of Bakunin's critique of Marx was founded on nothing more than a familiar baggage of romantic notions and nationalist prejudice, tightly bound together in a complex symmetry of logical relationships which he had learnt from German metaphysics, and lightly camouflaged by the banners of socialism and liberty.[30]

Such scholastic verbiage is a good indication of the political illiteracy and poverty of much contemporary liberal thought.

NOTES

1. Marx, K. et al. 1972. *Anarchism and Anarcho-Syndicalism.* Moscow: Progress Publishers, p. 149.
2. Dolgoff, S., ed., trans., introd., 1973. *Bakunin on Anarchy,* New York: Knopf, p. 334.
3. Dolgoff, op. cit., p. 294.
4. Kelly, A. 1982. *Mikhail Bakunin: A Study in the Psychology and Politics of Utopianism.* Oxford: Clarendon Press, pp. 151-58.
5. Dolgoff, op. cit., p. 346.
6. Dolgoff, op. cit., p. 197.
7. Maximoff, G. P. 1953. ed., *The Political Philosophy of Bakunin: Scientific Anarchism.* Glencoe: Free Press, p. 391.
8. Cole, G.D.H., 1954. *History of Socialist Thought, Vol. II, Marxism and Anarchism 1850-1890.* London: Macmillan, p. 230.
9. Harrison, J. F. 1983 *The Modern State; An Anarchist Analysis.* Montreal: Black Rose Books, p. 87.
10. Avrich, P. 1988, *Anarchist Portraits,* Princeton, New Jersey: Princeton University Press, pp. 8-9.
11. Lehning, A. 1973. *Michael Bakunin: Selected Writings.* London: Cape, p. 268.
12. Dolgoff, op. cit., p. 331.
13. Dolgoff, op. cit., p. 331.
14. Dolgoff, op. cit., p. 319.
15. Dolgoff, op. cit., p. 300
16. Dolgoff, op. cit., pp. 336-37.
17. Dolgoff, op. cit., p. 338.
18. Dolgoff, op. cit., p. 295.
19. Maximoff, op. cit., pp. 76-80.
20. Dolgoff, op. cit., p. 327.
21. Draper, H. 1978. *Karl Marx's Theory of Revolution.* New York: Monthly Review Press, pp. 568-9.
22. Cahm, J. C. 1978. "Bakunin." In E. Cahm & V. C. Fisera (1978) *Socialism and Nationalism. Vol. 1.* Nottingham: Spokesman Books, p. 42.
23. Dolgoff, op. cit., p. 341.
24. Dolgoff, op. cit., p. 341.
25. Cahm, op. cit., p. 47.
26. Clark, J. 1984. *The Anarchist Movement.* Montreal: Black Rose Books, pp. 89-93.
27. Draper, op. cit., p. 26.
28. Marx, K. 1973. *The Revolutions of 1848,* introduction and edited by D. Fernbach, Harmondsworth: Penguin, pp. 319-330.
29. Carter, Alan B. 1988. *Marx—A Radical Critique.* Brighton: Wheatsheaf, p. 219.
30. Kelly, op. cit., p. 220.

Chapter 15

Theory of Social Revolution

BAKUNIN has long been seen by both Marxist and liberal critics as an advocate of "pan-destructionism." He richly deserved, Eugène Pyziur writes, the epithet of "apostle of pan-destruction" for he elevated destruction to the rank of a programme.[1] Draper seems to see Bakunin as little more than a revolutionary brigand, and an advocate of elitist despotism involving pillage, theft and murder.[2] Bakunin has equally been portrayed as a millenarian visionary. While Marx was involved in the real revolution in establishing a "centralized organization," all that Bakunin had, Lichtheim writes, was a "chiliastic vision of an armed rising that would smash State and society"[3]— society, too, showing how little Lichtheim understood Bakunin's anarchism. Kelly as well writes of Bakunin's mystical anarchism and his millenarian vision of liberty and wholeness,[4] following the path of her mentor Isaiah Berlin who also wrote of Bakunin's apocalyptic vision.[5] The notion that Bakunin was some visionary utopian idealist bent on mass destruction has gone hand-in-hand with the idea that Bakunin believed that a revolution could simply be achieved by a spontaneous act of "will." Uncritically accepting Marx's own estimate, Paul Thomas writes: "Bakunin's extreme voluntarism takes the form of what is surely an overestimation of the potency of the revolutionary will among society's lower depths and outcasts."[6]

Yet, when one reads Bakunin it comes as a surprise that there is very little about destruction, in the sense of pillage, armed uprisings, assassination and the like; what he does offer is a sustained and reasoned critique of the three primary institutions of the contemporary world: the State, capitalism and religion, and the ideologies that support them, principally liberalism and Marxism. He advocated revolution, but he insists that this is a social revolution, and though he does speak of the destruction of the State and an end to economic serfdom through a revolutionary insurrection of the masses, he sees this process as less concerned with the advocacy of violence than in putting an end to violence. And the revolution for Bakunin is not only destructive of institutions, but also a creative process, allowing for the emergence and flourishing of pre-existing social organizations. As he writes:

It is this old system of organization based upon force that the social revolution should put an end to by giving full liberty to the masses, groups, communes, associations, and likewise to individuals themselves, and by destroying once and for all the historic cause of all violence, the power and the very existence of the State.[7]

Bakunin's critics, Marxists and liberals alike, have almost apoplexy at his suggestion that brigands may have revolutionary potential, but the violence of the State seemingly disappears by a process of amnesia.

How did Bakunin envisage the social revolution? The first thing that must be said is that he saw this revolution as springing from deep within the human psyche, for the instinct to revolt, Bakunin postulated as an important human faculty. The history of mankind is the history of the negation of the past, for the origins of the human species and of culture he sees as linked to the act of rebellion. Throughout human history, therefore, human beings have rebelled against oppression and unsatisfactory conditions. To revolt, Bakunin writes, "is a natural tendency of life. Even a worm turns against the foot that crushed it. In general the vitality and relative dignity of an animal can be measured by the intensity of its instinct to revolt." And he continues:

I contend that there has never existed a people so depraved that they did not at some time, at least at the beginning of their history, revolt against the yoke of their slave drivers and their exploiters, and against the yoke of the State.[8]

But the "negative passion" in itself did not make a social revolution, nor in themselves did suffering and oppression. He writes in *Statism and Anarchy* that when a man is driven to desperation,

he is then more likely to rebel. Despair is a bitter, passionate feeling capable of rousing men from their semiconscious resignation if they have already an idea of a more desirable situation. But poverty and desperation are still not sufficient to generate a social revolution. They may be able to call forth intermittent local rebellions, but not great and widespread uprisings.[9]

For this to happen people need to be inspired by a universal ideal.

Regarding the conditions and factors conducive to a social revolution, Bakunin makes a number of observations, particularly in examining the possibilities of revolution in Italy and Russia. We can consider each of these in turn.

Firstly, Bakunin stresses the importance of strikes in awakening the spirit of revolt among the workers. He writes:

> Who does not know what every single strike means to the workers in terms of suffering and sacrifices? But strikes are necessary; indeed they are necessary to such an extent that without them it would be impossible to arouse the masses from social struggle, nor would it be possible to have them organized. Strikes awaken in the masses all the social revolutionary instincts which reside deeply in the heart of every worker . . . When those instincts, stimulated by economic struggle awaken . . . the propaganda of social-revolutionary ideas become easy. For these ideas are simply the purest and most faithful expression of the instincts of the people . . . Every strike is the more valuable in that it broadens and deepens to an ever greater extent the gulf now separating the bourgeois class from the masses . . . There is no better means of detaching the workers from the political influence of the bourgeoisie than a strike.[10]

Bakunin therefore sees strikes as accentuating the struggle between labour and capital and as having enormous value in creating and organizing a form of workers' army. A general strike, he felt, in the conditions of that time, "now that the proletariat is deeply permeated with the ideas of emancipation, can only lead to a great cataclysm, which will regenerate society."[11] This great cataclysm necessarily implies, for Bakunin, a general insurrection by the people as a whole, for he never ceases to stress that the social revolution—a real and genuine revolution—is only that which is made by the people and not on behalf of the people.

Secondly, Bakunin denies that a social revolution could simply be made by the will of individuals, independent of social and economic circumstances. He was much less a voluntarist than his Marxist critics make out. Although like most nineteenth-century revolutionaries (Marx included), Bakunin had a feeling that the social revolution would be imminent—particularly in Italy—he was also aware that the social revolution would be a long process that may take many years for its realization. As he wrote in a letter to Nechaev (June 2, 1870):

> Popular revolutions are born by the actual force of events or else by the stress of history which flows unseen underground . . . It is impossible to bring about such a revolution artificially . . . There are some periods in history when revolutions are quite simply impossible; there are other periods when they are inevitable. In which of these periods do we now find ourselves? I am deeply convinced that we are in a period of universal, inevitable popular revolution . . . Will it break out soon, and where will it break first—in Russia, or in France, or in some other part of the west? No one can foretell. Maybe it will break out within a year . . . or not for ten or twenty years.[12]

Elsewhere he wrote:

> Revolutions are not improvised. They are not made at will by individuals. They came about through the force of circumstances and are independent of any deliberate will or conspiracy.[13]

Thirdly, Bakunin argued that a social revolution could never be genuine unless made by the people, and unless it went beyond a political revolution, using the term "political" as Bakunin used it, to mean coercive State institutions. Bakunin never denied the need for "organization," for the formation of workers' associations and trade unions, and he continually stressed the importance of class struggle against the bourgeoisie. It was necessary all over the world, he wrote, that "there should be pioneering groups or associations of advanced workers who were willing to initiate this great workers' movement of self-emancipation . . . the organization of the trade sections . . . bear in themselves the living seed of the new society which is to replace the old world. They are creating not only the ideas, but also the facts of the future itself."[14] The notion that Bakunin advocated simply "peasant socialism" or wished a return to some archaic past is simply untrue, and presents a travesty of his theory.

Bakunin therefore suggested that no political or nationalist revolution was sufficient in itself, and that a genuine revolution would be made by the people—peasants and urban workers in particular—who would destroy the bourgeois State thus allowing for the free federation of the workers and peasant associations and the local communities of the people. This did not imply the destruction of the whole "existing order," but essentially only of the institutions of property and the State. And the social revolution was not simply destructive but a creative act, a Hegelian negation, that allowed for the positive affirmation of existing social units, and the new forms of association that were coming into being. There are close affinities between the revolutionary perspectives of Marx and Bakunin, but whereas Marx saw the establishment of workers' associations and councils (soviets) as heralding and leading to the formation of a new workers' State (that would emerge as a counter-force to the bourgeoisie State), Bakunin saw the newly emerging workers' associations and the International itself, along with already pre-existing voluntary associations and "natural" social units, as forming the basis of an anarchist society. Some relevant extracts will illustrate Bakunin's essential thesis.

> No political or national revolution can ever triumph unless it is transformed into a social revolution, and unless the national revolution, precisely because of its radically socialist character, which is destructive of the State, becomes a universal revolution.
>
> Since the revolution must everywhere be achieved by the people, and since its supreme direction must always rest in the people, organized in a free federation of agricultural and industrial associations, the new revolutionary State, organized from the bottom up by revolutionary delegates ... will have as its chief objective the administration of public services, not the governing of peoples.[15]

These phrases are reminiscent of those of Saint-Simon, Weitling and of the Marxist notion of the "withering away" of the State, but Bakunin specifically repudiates any notion of State control, even during the period of revolutionary transition.

He also repudiates explicitly in this programme of the International Brotherhood (1869), from which this extract is taken, any idea of dictatorship or of a controlling or directing power within the revolution, or the idea that a secret society can make a revolution; the social revolution is made—indeed can only be made—by the people.

Elsewhere Bakunin writes:

> The way of the anarchist social revolution, which will come from the people themselves, is an elemental force

sweeping away all obstacles. Later, from the depths of the popular soul, there will spontaneously emerge the new creative forms of life.[16]

But Bakunin was critical of those—whether socialists or disciples of Hegel—who created ideal schemes of a new socialist society. There were in fact two paths, he suggested, to revolution; one is that of the utopian socialists who attempted to establish rural colonies based on socialist principles, thereby hoping in a gradual peaceful way, to initiate a radical transformation of society. But experiences over the last twenty years or so, in America and elsewhere, had proved that this was not a viable option. The other path is by a "general uprising of the people"—this Bakunin felt was the only way to achieve a social revolution. He envisaged both peasants and workers as the most important elements in this transformation. As Bakunin wrote in his circular to his Italian friends:

> Organize the city proletariat in the name of revolutionary socialism and in doing this, unite it into one preparatory organization together with the peasants. An uprising by the proletariat alone would not be enough; with that we would have only a political revolution which would necessarily produce a natural and legitimate reaction on the part of the peasants ... Only a wide-sweeping revolution embracing both the city workers and peasants would be sufficiently strong to overthrow and break the organized power of the State, backed as it is by all the resources of the possessing classes. But an all-embracing, that is, a social revolution, is a simultaneous revolution of the people of the cities and of the peasantry.[17]

In stressing the solidarity of the peasants and urban workers in overthrowing the State, and in suggesting the necessity of turning a bourgeois political revolution into a social revolution, Bakunin has often been seen as a precursor of Lenin and the Bolsheviks. Although they did indeed follow a similar strategy, their aims were quite dissimilar to those of Bakunin, for Lenin followed the essence of Marx's theory, and established by the "seizure" of State power, a workers' State. But as Bakunin indeed predicted (so his arguments against Marxism have more than a purely theoretical significance), this only led to another despotism, and at the end of the social revolution.

Fourthly, in his discussion on the possibilities of revolution in Russia, Bakunin suggested that the "brigand" also has a part to play. In his letter to Nechaev he wrote that there were three facets of Russian peasant life that had potential for a revolution. One was the frequent uprisings among the peasantry. Another was the Russian commune, which though weakened by patriarchy and isolation, had a socialist basis. The third element was brigandage, which, he wrote, contained in itself a "protest both against the State and against the restrictions of a patriarchal society."[18] In *Statism and Anarchy*, he wrote, "brigandage is an important historical phenomenon in Russia; the first rebels, the first revolutionists in Russia, Pugachev and Stenka Razin, were brigands."[19] Peasant rebellions were indeed common throughout the nineteenth century. There were around 1,200 peasant uprisings in Russia between 1825 and 1861, all put down punitively by the Tsarist authorities, and brigandage was still an important phenomenon. Bakunin thought of the peasant bandits as having a role in co-ordinating the separate communal uprisings, as acting as kind of "channels" or "forerunners" of the revolution. Bakunin undoubtedly idealized the peasant bandits, but whether this allows one to describe Bakunin as a classic example of a markedly "archaic and romantic" revolutionary is questionable.[20] There is more to Bakunin than an advocacy of banditry. But of course his defence of brigands has always proved good ammunition for his opponents. Kelly writes that Bakunin's presentation of the bandits as "the noble and heroic spearhead of a popular revolution was pure fantasy,"[21] and Draper implies that Bakunin thought of the brigand as the "only true revolutionary," and this entailed his advocacy of pillage and murder.[22] On this issue Bakunin wrote:

> And which of us is not a robber or thief? Isn't that what the government is? And what about our government and private speculators and businessmen? Or our landowners and merchants. I personally cannot stand either robbery or violence, or in fact anything that constitutes an assault on humanity, but I admit that if I had to choose between the robbery and the violence that sits on a throne or makes use of every possible privilege, and the robbery and violence of the people, then I would not have the slightest hesitation in coming down on the side of the latter. I admit that from the point of view of real humanitarianism the world of popular brigands is far, far from beautiful. But what is beautiful in Russia? What can be more filthy than our respectable, hierarchical world of

middle class civilization and cleanliness, with its smooth Western facade hiding the most awful debauchery?[23]

In the repressive, awful conditions of Tsarist Russia, brigandage, Bakunin writes, is the only way out for the individual, and a mass uprising—the social revolution—for the people.[24] Going to the brigands doesn't mean sharing their aims and actions, which are frequently vile; it means instilling them with a new spirit and a new world outlook.[25] And it is worth noting that while Bakunin is often seen as having had an important influence on Russian populists, he never advocated, as did the populists, the assassination of people. But like other anarchists, he did not revile those, who, in the intolerable situation of nineteenth-century Russia, had made recourse to such methods.

Bakunin did not directly advocate violence, any more than did Marx, but he realized that any revolution would inevitably entail the destruction of life and property. "Revolutions are not child's play" he wrote. And a popular insurrection is, by its very nature, "instinctive, chaotic and destructive and always entails great personal sacrifice and an enormous loss of public and private property."[26] But although Bakunin stresses that a revolution will entail widespread destruction, it must be kept in mind that Bakunin was fundamentally a social thinker, and he was primarily concerned with the destruction of institutions—of the State and private property—rather than of people. "There can be no revolution," he wrote, "without a sweeping and passionate destruction . . . since by means of such destruction new worlds are born and come into existence."[27] Such phrases make sense not in apocalyptic terms, although they do have an apocalyptic ring about them, but only in sociological terms, implying a radical social transformation.

A final aspect of Bakunin's theory of social revolution concerns his advocacy of a secret revolutionary society that would be a "collective, invisible dictatorship" within the revolution. His writings and the programmatic statements on "secret societies," especially his earlier ones, have given the impression to many scholars that although Bakunin preached a libertarian doctrine, anarchism, he was at heart, and also in theory, also an advocate of a revolutionary dictatorship, and thus "despotism." For this reason, Marxists have dismissed Bakunin as an irrelevant and dangerous romantic, while liberals have equated Bakunin with Robespierre and the Jacobins and considered him as a precursor of Bolshevism, or even Stalinism. I will quote a few typical examples.

Regarding anarchists as having a choice only between "impotent and meaningless rhetoric" and "elitist despotism"—thereby displaying an incredible ignorance of the real anarchist movement—Hal Draper uses Bakunin's writings on "secret societies" to argue that the crux of Bakunin's political philosophy was a belief in "the dictatorship of the intelligentsia." Bakunin's ideas, Draper contends, have their roots in "Jacobin-communist conspiratorialism" (on this he agrees with the liberals), and all Bakunin and his secret band of conspirators were concerned with was to "impose" their hidden control over the supposed social revolution. He also accepts that Bakunin was concerned both to "destroy" and to take over the control, "as dictator," of the International Working Men's Association. Draper comes to these conclusions by an incredible distortion of the substance of what Bakunin was trying to convey in his letters to Richard and Nechaev, and by accepting Engels and Lafargue's pamphlet on the "Alliance" (1873) as if it were the gospel truth.[28]

Following Carr, Eugène Pyziur stresses that Bakunin's political philosophy contained completely contradictory elements: anarchism and a stress on liberty, and the advocacy of a secret society. The latter, with its exclusiveness and conspiratorial character, and in its emphasis on discipline, was the "mode," of the modern totalitarian party. Thus, Bakunin is seen by Pyziur as a precursor of Bolshevism. Bakunin's political philosophy, he concludes, combined anarchism with a struggle for unlimited power. He writes:

> In any endeavour to put into practice Bakunin's anarchism, the utopian elements, aimed at the securing of liberty, would not be realizable. The disciplinary elements, left unbalanced by other factors, would predominate incontestably. The culmination would be a total despotism.[29]

What strange logic!

Aileen Kelly provides us with an identical thesis, suggesting that Bakunin combined both anarchist and Jacobin strands in his political thought. Like Pyziur, she argues that the anarchist strand is essentially a millenarian vision; it implies a belief in "absolute liberty," and in the "idealization of the peasants," as well as a "romantic cult of primitive spontaneity" which Bakunin accepted with enthusiasm. The Jacobin strand, on the other hand, is linked by Kelly to Bakunin's writings on secret societies and to his conflict with Marx over the control of the International. She contends that Bakunin, in reality, had established a "centralized hierarchical organization"—Bakunin's Secret Alliance—

whose aim was to "direct" the International along lines laid down by Bakunin. His anarchism was simply a screen for Bakunin's lust for power, as Marx and Engels always alleged. And his writings on secret societies imply that Bakunin was concerned with establishing a dictatorship and to "impose" a revolution on the people from above—the people "would be liberated against their will."[30]

Thus, following earlier scholars like Steklov and Carr, Kelly emphasizes a fundamental contradiction between Bakunin's anarchy, and his theory of dictatorship and links both to Bakunin's yearning to identify himself with some absolute—the people. She concludes that the Stalinist State is an apt description of Bakunin's conception of revolution.

All three writers—Draper, Pyziur and Kelly—tend to overemphasize the role of secret societies in Bakunin's conception of the social revolution, and to interpret the meaning of the words used by Bakunin to describe his conception of an "invisible dictatorship" (particularly as expressed in his letters to Richard and Nechaev), in the most negative and damaging way possible. Part of the problem is that the word "dictatorship" nowadays, after the fascist dictatorships of Mussolini and Hitler, carries such a loaded meaning. But although the assessments of Bakunin are, I think, extremely biased and give a misleading interpretation of what Bakunin was trying to conceptualize, nevertheless, there is a sense in which his advocacy of a secret revolutionary society does not accord well with his anarchism. Clark is essentially correct in suggesting that Bakunin's belief in the importance of secret associations and small groups of advanced militants indicates a strong vanguardist undercurrent in his thought, "though it is neither so central to his outlook as his opponents allege, nor so trivial and innocuous as some of his defenders claim."[31]

It has to be recognized that discussion of Bakunin's secret societies and the Alliance of Socialist Democracy relate to three distinct entities. First, there is the Alliance itself, which was not a secret society, but an open section within the International, made up largely, but not exclusively, of devotees of Bakunin's libertarian socialism. There were many, besides Bakunin, who wanted the International Working Men's Associations to be based on federal principles, and were critical of the idea of making the General Council into a executive directory. Bakunin drew a distinction between the International and the Alliance, and saw them as having different functions. As Bakunin put it:

> The Alliance is the necessary complement to the International. But the International and the Alliance, while

having the same ultimate aims, perform different functions. The International endeavours to unify the working
masses . . . regardless of nationality or religious and
political beliefs, into one compact body: the Alliance, on
the other hand, tries to give these masses a really revolutionary direction.[32]

The Marxist accusation that Bakunin wanted to destroy the International, become its dictator or replace the programme of International—
which was vague to say the least—with that of the Alliance are all
unfounded. And Bakunin's distinction between the International and
the Alliance does not accord with the suggestion made by Carr that
while Bakunin wanted the International to be an anarchist association
(which is true in a sense), the Alliance was simply a select and secret
revolutionary group exercising a "collective dictatorship" over the forces of the revolution.[33]

Secondly, there are the various small groups of the devotees that
gathered around Bakunin to form the Revolutionary Brotherhood, and
which formed the nucleus of the Alliance. But this was little more than
a loosely knit group of associates, all showing a commitment to anarchism. Given the need for secrecy and the fact that Bakunin certainly
felt the need for a network of cadres who would form a vanguard association to support the revolution, this by no means implied the existence of a tightly-knit conspiratorial group under Bakunin's dictatorship. Bakunin had a dominant personality, but his temperament and
life style made him a highly unlikely person to organize a functioning
conspiratorial group on par with that of the Jesuits. Bakunin's supposed secret societies never functioned as organizations of any real
consequence. Indeed, Bakunin's friend Guillaume, in his history of the
International, writes of Bakunin painting "a picture of an organization
which existed only theoretically in Bakunin's brain as a kind of dream
indulged in with delight, a chimera formed in the clouds of his
cigarette smoke."[34] The notion of a secret Alliance seems to have largely
been a figment of Bakunin's—and Marx's—imagination.

Thirdly, there are the writings of Bakunin, his draft proposals of the
principles and organization for the various International Brotherhoods
that he concocted, and his letters to Richard and Nechaev, together
which outline the aims and purposes of a secret society. The fact that
these societies never in reality functioned is beside the point; the writings indicate Bakunin's thoughts on what he felt was a necessary factor
to generate a social revolution.

For Bakunin, neither poverty nor despair, nor socio-economic conditions, nor the capture of State power can in themselves lead to a social revolution—it can only be achieved by the organization of the masses which will "break down the power of the bourgeoisie and the State, and lay the ground for a new world."[35] Organizing the popular forces to carry out the revolution, such is the only task, he wrote, of those who sincerely aim at the emancipation of humanity. Bakunin therefore placed an important role on organization and the development of the revolutionary ideal. A revolution can take place, he wrote, "only when the people are stirred by a universal idea, are evolved historically from the depths of popular instincts ... when this ideal and this popular faith meet poverty of the sort that drives man to desperation; then the social revolution is near and inevitable."[36]

It is in the propagating of this ideal that Bakunin's conception of a secret society comes into play. In his letters to Richard and Nechaev, the function of this society and the kind of dictatorship it was to wield is clearly spelt out by Bakunin, and some relevant extracts seem appropriate, given the interpretation or rather misinterpretation they have been given.

Anarchy, the mutiny of all local passions and the awakening of spontaneous life at all points, must be well developed in order for the revolution to remain alive, real and powerful. Once the revolution has won its first victory (i.e. the overthrow of State power) we (unlike the political revolutionaries) must foment, awaken and unleash all the passions, we must produce anarchy and, like invisible pilots in the thick of the popular tempest, we must not steer it by any open power but by the collective dictatorship of all the allies—a dictatorship without insignia, titles or official rights, and all the stronger for having none of the paraphernalia of power. That is the only dictatorship I accept.[37]

This is in a letter addressed to Albert Richard, who was a French anarchist from Lyons and who collaborated with the provisional government in 1870. Bakunin clearly had in mind a post-revolutionary situation, akin to that which had occurred during the French revolution. And, he feared that in this context, those revolutionaries like Danton and Robespierre who insisted on setting up "Committees of Public Safety" would inevitably betray the revolution, and lead to reaction.

His conception of a secret society therefore, which is to prepare and organize itself in advance of the revolution, is not to "impose" the revolution on the people, or liberate it against their will, still less to be a "dictatorship" (in the ordinary sense of this word), it is to continually agitate, "invisible" amongst the populace for anarchy—that is, for the self-management of the people. Nothing is further from the normal understanding of "dictatorship."

In his letter to Nechaev, Bakunin explicitly distinguishes his own ideas from Nechaev's conception of a revolution. You follow the Jesuitical teaching, he wrote to Nechaev, and systematically kill all individual, human feelings in the people and all their personal sense of justice. "You train them in lies, suspicion, espionage and denunciation, relying far more on the outward fetters with which you have chained them than on their inner virtue."[38] My system, Bakunin stresses to his ex-friend, "refutes not only the value, but even the possibility, of any revolution that is not spontaneous or popular and socialist . . . and therefore the sole object of a secret society must not be to create an artificial force outside the people, but to arouse, unite and organize the spontaneous popular forces; in this way, the only possible, the only effective army of revolution, is not outside the people, but consists of the people themselves."

And Bakunin continues:

> The organization (of the secret society) should only be the general headquarters of (the people's army) and the organizer not of its own, but of the people's forces, as a link between the people's instincts and revolutionary thought. But revolutionary thought is only revolutionary, alive, active and true in so far as it expresses, and only in so far as it formulates, popular instincts that have been worked out by history. Any effort to impose our ideas on the people which might be opposed to their instincts signifies a desire to enslave them to a new sovereignty . . . The organization must be sincerely impregnated with the idea that it is the servant and helper of the people, and by no means their ruler.[39]

Even in the midst of the revolution, the secret society should not alter its chief purpose and aim: "to help people towards self-determination on the lines of the most complete equality and the fullest human freedom in every direction, without the least interference from any sort of domination." Members of the secret society should renounce all official power, only influencing the people by a force that is invisible, the "collective dictatorship" of the organization.[40]

Only the most jaundiced scholar, or one blinded by extreme antipathy towards Bakunin or anarchism, could interpret these words as indicating that Bakunin's conception of a secret society implied a revolutionary dictatorship in the Jacobin sense, still less a "despotism" (which is a favourite word used by both liberals and Marxists to describe this aspect of Bakunin's philosophy). And it is clear too—with the experiences of the French revolution in mind—that Bakunin saw the secret society as less of a "vanguard" than a force which in the midst of the revolution would serve to safeguard the revolution from the forces of reaction, or from those radicals who might set themselves up as dictatorial "Committees of Public Safety." And this the secret society would do by "invisibly" and collectively supporting anarchy, the realization of the liberty of the people. Marxists have always stressed that a workers' State was necessary in the post-revolutionary period to counter the bourgeois reaction; Bakunin was also concerned to challenge this reaction, but he feared the Jacobin kind of government that would re-assert a new form of despotism. Kelly chided Bakunin's faith in the spontaneity and revolutionary potential of the masses. The Russian revolution essentially confirmed Bakunin's ideas of a social revolution, both in its origins and in the aftermath. As Sam Dolgoff writes:

> Bakunin's warnings to the Bolsheviks of his day, the Jacobins and the Blanquists, as to where their policies could lead, read almost like a preview of the Russian revolution from its inception to the final seizure of power and the establishment of a totalitarian State.[41]

Max Nomad's suggestion that Bolshevism was a "hybrid of Bakuninist activism and Marxist verbiage"[42] implying that Bakunin was a precursor of Lenin—a thesis strongly argued also by Pyziur—does Bakunin a gross and malicious injustice. Not Bakunin, but Robespierre, Blanqui and Tkachev, as Dolgoff suggests, are Lenin's real forebears. To what degree Lenin can be said to be true to the legacy of Marx has been disputed by some Marxists. But whatever the verdict, Blanqui, Marx and Lenin had much in common, and Bakunin in his advocacy of anarchism, libertarian socialism, was very different from all three revolutionaries.

The weakness of Bakunin's position regarding the social revolution is that, as Frank Harrison writes, he, like all anarchists appears to leave the door open for counterrevolution because of an unwillingness to accept the organizational measures necessary for combatting reaction.[43] It would seem that Bakunin's conception of a secret society was envisaged not only as a vanguard association to spread the revolutionary ideal through propaganda, but precisely as a measure to reserve and mobilize—as an invisible collective force—the anarchy of the postrevolutionary period.

Although Bakunin's writings on secret societies often seem to contradict his own anarchist principles, to stress this contradiction as the essence of Bakunin's thought, and to fail to contextualize what the real aims of these societies were, is to greatly distort Bakunin's message. Bakunin was no abstract Hegelian idealist playing around with words, and living in a fantasy world of his own making as Kelly portrays him. He was a sociologically informed revolutionary who had a sense of history and was trying to unravel the real problems of initiating and preserving a true and genuine social revolution. The revolution came in 1917, as spontaneously as Bakunin had anticipated—what happened in the aftermath certainly confirms the prescience of Bakunin's critique of Marxism.

But although the emphasis in Bakunin's writings is certainly on the destruction of the State and property relations, and this has been seen as a limitation of Bakunin's work (Emma Goldman certainly felt this), it is unfair to Bakunin to put too much stress on the "passion for destruction." For Bakunin saw this also as a "creative passion" and there is ample evidence that he had some very significant proposals to make on the nature of the social revolution and of the future anarchist society.

NOTES

1. Pyziur, E. 1955. *The Doctrine of Anarchism of Michael Bakunin,* Milwaukee: Regnery, p. 3.
2. Draper, H. 1978. *Karl Marx's Theory of Revolution.* New York: Monthly Review Press, p. 292.
3. Lichtheim, G. 1970. *A Short History of Socialism.* London: Weidenfeld & Nicolson, p. 128.
4. Kelly, A. 1982. *Mikhail Bakunin: A Study in the Psychology and Politics of Utopianism.* Oxford: Clarendon Press, p. 22.
5. Berlin, I. 1978. *Russian Thinkers.* Harmondsworth, Penguin, p. 103.
6. Thomas, P. 1980. *Karl Marx and the Anarchists.* London: Routledge & Kegan Paul, p. 341.
7. Maximoff, G. P. 1953. ed., *The Political Philosophy of Bakunin: Scientific Anarchism.* Glencoe: Free Press, p. 373.

8.　Dolgoff, S. 1973. ed., trans, introd., *Bakunin on Anarchy*, New York: Knopf, pp. 308-9.
9.　Dolgoff, op. cit., p. 335.
10.　Maximoff, op. cit., p. 384.
11.　Maximoff, op. cit., p. 383.
12.　Lehning, A. 1973. *Michael Bakunin: Selected Writings*. London: Cape, p. 183.
13.　Pyziur, op. cit., p. 68.
14.　Dolgoff, op. cit., p. 352-5.
15.　Dolgoff, op. cit., p. 15.
16.　Dolgoff, op. cit., p. 325.
17.　Maximoff, op. cit., p. 378-9.
18.　Lehning, op. cit., p. 185.
19.　Dolgoff, op. cit., p. 347.
20.　cf. Hobsbawm, E.J. 1959. *Primitive Rebels*, Manchester: Manchester University Press, p. 165.
21.　Kelly, op. cit., p. 216.
22.　Draper, op. cit., p. 292.
23.　Lehning, op. cit., p. 186.
24.　Dolgoff, op. cit., p. 347.
25.　Lehning, op. cit., p. 187.
26.　Dolgoff, op. cit., p. 334.
27.　Maximoff, op. cit., p. 381.
28.　Draper, op. cit., pp. 564-569; Draper, H. 1986. *Karl Marx's Theory of Revolution, Vol. III, The Dictatorship of the Proletariat*, New York: Monthly Review Press, pp. 93-98.
29.　Pyziur, op. cit., p. 146.
30.　Kelly, op. cit., pp. 237-249.
31.　Clark, J. 1984. *The Anarchist Moment*. Montreal: Black Rose Books, p. 73.
32.　Dolgoff, op. cit., p. 157.
33.　Carr, E. H. 1937. *Michael Bakunin*, New York: Knopf, p. 440.
34.　Carr, op. cit., p. 439.
35.　Maximoff, op. cit., p. 385.
36.　Pyziur, op. cit., p. 69-70.
37.　Lehning, op. cit., p. 180.
38.　Lehning, op. cit., p. 190.
39.　Lehning, op. cit., p. 190-191.
40.　Lehning, op. cit., p. 182-92.
41.　Dolgoff, op. cit., p. 16.
42.　Nomad, M. 1933. *Apostles of Revolution*. New York: Collier, p. 213.
43.　Harrison, J. F. 1983. *The Modern State: An Anarchist Analysis*. Montreal: Black Rose Books, p. 113.

Chapter 16

Conclusion

BAKUNIN was a holistic thinker. As Pyziur writes, his radicalism was dominated by a desire "to achieve a unity of theory and practice, of fact and value, of thought and action, within the reality of a given historical social order."[1] He opposed all the dualisms which Western culture had bequeathed from mechanistic philosophy and bourgeois political theory, particularly the oppositions between individual and society, philosophy and empirical knowledge, nature and humans. But such a holism did not imply that Bakunin envisaged the dissolution of the personality in some mystical union with the absolute. "The yearning to identify with a universal, omnipotent force, to feel oneself entrusted with a historical mission," writes Kelly, "is the emotional core of totalitarian movements."[2] Bakunin had no such mystical yearning and he was too much of an anarchist, and he had learnt his lessons well from "good old Hegel" (whom Kelly clearly does not understand) to think of "the merging of consciousness and will with a transcendental whole"—the absolute, which Kelly suggests for Bakunin is the idealized "people." Bakunin was concerned with holism but not this kind of mystical union. What he was concerned with was to overcome the dualism by the creation of a society that would acknowledge our interdependence with nature, and that would also allow for the full liberty and sociality of the human person. He was both a historical materialist and a social anarchist.

Bakunin was the true apostle of anarchism. He had an enormous influence on the whole anarchist movement that emerged in the closing decades of the nineteenth century. Indeed, in an important sense it was Bakunin who laid the foundations for the development of anarchism, as a social movement, independent of both reformist socialism and Marxism. Bakunin had a profound influence on the anarchist movement and on working class politics in Italy, Switzerland, Spain and several Latin American countries. His "collectivist" anarchism, though never presented in a systematic fashion, was the first outline of a libertarian socialist theory that combined liberalism, socialism and atheism into a coherent theory. This theory was subsequently developed by Kropotkin, Reclus, Cafiero and Malatesta. There are, of course, many gaps and limitations in Bakunin's theory. He had no developed ecological theory, though it was there in embryonic form. He had, like many of his contemporaries, deep racial and national prejudices that often marred his judgement, and distorted his socialist perspective. He had a passion for "secret societies" which as Reclus argued, had no part in anarchism. He had no developed theory of gender and seemed unconcerned with sexual liberation, although he clearly accepted gender equality and also expressed hostility towards patriarchy. He described the Russian peasant family as a "whitewashed graveyard" and was critical of the "despotism" of the husband and father within the family.[3]

In this regard, it is worth citing from Kropotkin's memoirs. Kropotkin visited the Jura mountains in the early 1870s meeting Guillaume, Schwirtzguebel and other associates of Bakunin. The impression one gets from Kropotkin's work is that Bakunin, far from being dictatorial, was seen as a great "moral personality," warmly held in high esteem by his comrades. Bakunin, he writes, was never treated as an authority. "I only once heard," Kropotkin recalled, "Bakunin's name invoked as an authority in itself and that impresses me so deeply that I even now remember the spot where the conversation took place and all the surroundings. Some young men were indulging in talk that was not very respectful toward the other sex, when one of the women who were present put a sudden stop to it by exclaiming: 'Pity that Michel is not here; he would put you in your place!'"[4]

But what gives Bakunin his contemporary relevance is not only his writings on anarchism, but his important critiques of liberalism and Marxism. Even Max Nomad, who was no friend of Bakunin, could acknowledge that in his critique of Marx, Bakunin showed himself to be "a penetrating thinker and prophet" who raised problems with Marxist theory that Marx was unable or unwilling to see.[5]

At a time when many see Marxism as the only radical alternative to corporate capitalism—and Marxism and liberalism between them seem to have intellectual hegemony—the writings of Bakunin have a special significance. It does not bode well to dismiss Bakunin, as do Marxists and liberals, as a historical curiosity, for his ideas have a freshness and originality and a contemporary relevance which we would do well to examine and learn from. As Sam Dolgoff concluded in a reexamination of the libertarian socialist tradition, "much can still be learned from the failures as well as the achievements of Bakunin and the other pioneers who fought for freedom a century ago."[6]

NOTES

1. Pyziur, E. 1955. *The Doctrine of Anarchism of Michael Bakunin*, Milwaukee: Regnery, p. 53.
2. Kelly, A. 1982. *Mikhail Bakunin: A Study in the Psychology and Politics of Utopianism*. Oxford: Clarendon Press, p. 255.
3. Dolgoff, S. 1973. ed., trans, introd., *Bakunin on Anarchy*, New York: Knopf, p. 346.
4. Kropotkin, P., 1989, *Memoirs of a Revolutionist*, Montreal: Black Rose Books, p. 289.
5. Nomad, M. 1933. *Apostles of Revolution*. New York: Collier, p. 192.
6. Dolgoff, op. cit., p. 21.

Bibliography

Aldred, G. A. 1940. *Bakunin* (pamphlet), 68 pp. Glasgow: Strickland Press.

Avrich, P. 1974, *Bakunin and Nechaev*, London: Freedom Press

Avrich, P. 1978. *The Russian Anarchists*. New York: Norton.

Avrich, P. 1988, *Anarchist Portraits*, Princeton, New Jersey: Princeton University Press.

Berlin, I. 1978. *Russian Thinkers*. Harmondsworth, Penguin.

Cahm, J. C. 1978. "Bakunin." In E. Cahm & V. C. Fisera (1978) *Socialism and Nationalism. Vol. 1.* Nottingham: Spokesman Books, pp. 33-49.

Carr, E. H. 1937. *Michael Bakunin.* New York: Knopf.

Carter, Alan B. 1988. *Marx—A Radical Critique.* Brighton: Wheatsheaf.

Clark, J. 1984. *The Anarchist Moment.* Montreal: Black Rose Books.

Cole, G.D.H., 1954. *History of Socialist Thought, Vol. II, Marxism and Anarchism 1850-1890.* London: Macmillan.

Dolgoff, S., ed., trans, introd., 1973. *Bakunin on Anarchy.* New York: Knopf.

Draper, H. 1978. *Karl Marx's Theory of Revolution, Vol II, The Politics of Social Classes.* New York: Monthly Review Press.

Draper, H. 1986. *Karl Marx's Theory of Revolution, Vol. III, The Dictatorship of the Proletariat,* New York: Monthly Review Press.

Fleming, M. 1979. *The Anarchist Way to Socialism: Elisée Reclus and 19th Century European Anarchism.* London: Croom Helm.

Fromm, E. 1962. *Beyond the Chains of Illusion.* London: Sphere Books.

Gray, A. 1946. *The Socialist Tradition: Moses to Lenin.* London: Longmans.

Guerin, D. 1986. "From Proudhon to Bakunin," *Our Generation* 17/2: pp. 23-34.

Harrison, J. F. 1983. *The Modern State: An Anarchist Analysis.* Montreal: Black Rose Books.

Hobsbawm, E.J. 1959. *Primitive Rebels,* Manchester: Manchester University Press.

Hostetter, R. 1958. *The Italian Socialist Movement.* Princeton, NJ: Van Nostrand.

Jacoby, R. 1975. *Social Amnesia: A Critique of Conformist Psychologists from Adler to Laing.* Boston: Beacon Press.

Jou. J. 1964. *The Anarchists,* London: Methuen.

Kelly, A. 1982. *Mikhail Bakunin: A Study in the Psychology and Politics of Utopianism.* Oxford: Clarendon Press.

Kramnick, I. 1972. "On Anarchism and the Real World: William Godwin and Radical England," *American Political Science Review,* 66, pp. 114-128.

Kropotkin, P., 1989, *Memoirs of a Revolutionist,* Montreal: Black Rose Books.

Lampert, E. 1957. *Studies in Rebellion.* London: Routledge & Kegan Paul.

Lehning, A. 1973. *Michael Bakunin: Selected Writings.* London: Cape.

Lichtheim, G. 1970. *A Short History of Socialism.* London: Weidenfeld & Nicolson.

Marx, K. 1973. *The Revolutions of 1848,* introduction and edited by D. Fernbach, Harmondsworth: Penguin.

Marx, K. & Engels, F. 1968. *Selected Works.* London: Lawrence & Wishort.

Marx, K. et al. 1972. *Anarchism and Anarcho-Syndicalism.* Moscow: Progress Publishers.

Masters, A. 1974. *Bakunin: The Father of Anarchism.* London: Sidgwich and Jackson.

Maximoff, G. P., ed., 1953. *The Political Philosophy of Bakunin: Scientific Anarchism.* Glencoe: Free Press.

McLelland, D. 1973. *Karl Marx: His Life and Thought.* London: Macmillan.

Mehring, F. 1936. *Karl Marx: His Life and Thought,* London: Macmillan.

Munck, R. 1986. *The Difficult Dialogue: Marxism and Nationalism.* London: Zed Books.

Nettlau, M. 1976. *Writings on Bakunin.* London: C. Slienger

Nomad, M. 1933. *Apostles of Revolution.* New York: Collier.

Pengam, A. 1987. "Anarcho-Communism." In M. Rubel & J. Crump (eds.). *Non-Market Socialism in the 19th and 20th Centuries.* London: MacMillan, pp. 60-82.

Pyziur, E. 1955. *The Doctrine of Anarchism of Michael Bakunin.* Milwaukee: Regnery.

Rubel, M. 1987. *Non-Market Socialism in the Nineteenth Century.* In M. Rubel & J. Crump. op. cit., pp. 10-34.

Thomas, P. 1980. *Karl Marx and the Anarchists.* London: Routledge & Kegan Paul.

Thomson, D. 1964. *Democracy in France Since 1870.* Oxford University Press.

Ulam, A. 1965. *Lenin and the Bolsheviks.* London: Collins/Fontana.

Venturi, F. 1960. *Roots of Revolution: A History of Populist & Socialist Movements in 19th Century Russia.* Trans. F. Haskell. University of Chicago Press.

Woodcock, G. 1962. *Anarchism.* Harmondsworth: Penguin.

Index

Avrich, Paul, 128
Bakunin, Michael
  accused of being Russian spy, 42;
  attends Geneva congress, 35-37;
  critique of Marxism (state
  socialism) 117-124, 125-134; critique of Mazzini, 54-56; critique of
  Rousseau, 86-87; critique of the
  State, 96-104; early life, 5-18;
  exile in Siberia, 22-23; his anti-
  Semitism, 42; his atheism, 102-
  103; his collectivist anarchism,
  76; his federalism, 112; his
  Hegelianism, 7-8; his last years,
  65-68; his pan-Slavism, 6, 25; his
  theory of revolution, 136-150;
  imprisonment, 18, 20-22; marriage, 22; on capitalism, 99, 105-
  107; on nationalism, 131-132; on
  peasantry, 121; on secret
  societies, 143-149; on science,
  130-131; on socialism, 105-115;
  on the Paris Commune, 111-112;
  on the proletariat, 121-123; on
  the revolution in Lyons, 48-49;
  personality, 1-4; relations with
  Herzen, 26-28; relations with
  Marx, 17-18, 28-29, 37-40, 60-64,
  66, 105; relations with mother,
  22; relations with Nechaev, 43-
  46; relations with Proudhon, 12-
  13, 108; relations with wife
  Antonia, 22-23, 27, 34, 65, 67-68;
  sexual impotence, 22; social
  theory, 89-95.

Becker, Johann, 37
Beethoven, Ludwig, 18
Belinsky, Vissarion, 4, 6, 7-8, 11
Berlin, Isaiah, 71-73, 89-90, 93-94
Blanc, Louis, 108
Blanqui, Auguste, 28, 40, 106, 149
Blanquists, 31, 53, 60, 62
Bolshevism, 4, 141
bourgeoisie, 17
brigands, 142-143
Bright, John, 34
Cabet, Etienne, 12, 108

capitalism, 99, 101, 106
Cafiero, Carlo, 50, 56, 67, 152
Cahm, Caroline, 131-132
Carr, E. H., 1, 4, 5, 7, 11, 14, 17, 22, 24,
  26, 38, 60, 74, 93, 144, 146
Carter, Alan, 134
Clark, John, 117-118
Cole, G. D. H., 2, 28, 51, 53, 59, 92, 113,
  119, 121-122, 127
communism, 11, 133
Comte, Auguste, 78, 82
Darwin, Charles, 78
Decembrist revolt of 1825, 5, 26
Descartes, Rene, 119
dialectical method, 7
Dolgoff, Sam, 149, 153
Draper, Hal, 131, 133, 144
Durkheim, Emile, 88, 93
Engels, Friedrich, 9, 15, 62, 65, 67, 122,
  133
enlightenment philosophy, 79
Fanelli, Giuseppe, 56
Feuerbach, Ludwig, 9, 76, 82-83
Fichte, 6, 7
Fourier, Charles, 11, 106, 108
Freemasonry, 30
French encyclopedists, 6
French revolution, 16
Fromm, Erich, 86, 90

Gambuzzi, Carlo, 34
Garibaldi, Giuseppe, 34-35
God, 30, 83, 89, 103
Godwin, William, 80
Gray, Alexander, 83, 91
Guerin, Daniel, 13
Guillaume, James, 21, 29, 38, 47, 52,
  55-56, 59-60, 62, 68, 146, 153

Harrison, Frank, 149-150
Hegel, Wilhelm F., 6, 7, 9, 12, 75, 76, 78,
  88, 118
Hegelian philosophy, 7, 10, 14, 79, 93
Herwegh, Georg, 11, 12
Herzen, Alexander, 1-2, 6, 8, 23, 24, 25,
  27, 42, 45, 71-74
Hess, Moses, 42
historical materialism, 78-84

157

The Collected Works of Peter Kropotkin

The Collected Works of Peter Kropotkin (1842-1921) will be published by Black Rose Books over the next four years. Each volume is introduced by George Woodcock. The collection will contain some twelve volumes, including a companion biography written by George Woodcock and Ivan Avakumovic.

ISSN: 1188-5807

already published in the series ...

MEMOIRS OF A REVOLUTIONIST *(Volume 1)*

This precious account tells the story of the dramatic conversion from Russian prince to dedicated anarchist. Provides a study of the early anarchist movement and an extraordinary portrait of the old Russia of Kropotkin's youth.

504p ISBN: 0-921689-18-7 $19.95 (pbk.) / ISBN: 0-921689-19-5 $39.95 (bound)

THE GREAT FRENCH REVOLUTION *(Volume 2)*

Kropotkin analyzes the drama of the French Revolution not only as a complex interplay of leading personalities or as a chain of political decisions made from above, but describes a great reordering of the economic bases of the ancient regime by the mass of urban workers and the peasantry.

630p ISBN: 0-921689-38-1 $19.95 (pbk.) / ISBN: 0-921689-39-X $38.95 (bound)

MUTUAL AID: *A FACTOR OF EVOLUTION (Volume 3)*

First published in 1903, Kropotkin counters T.H. Huxley's argument that evolution is propelled by a ruthless struggle for existence with the argument that in nature cooperation is as important as competition.

362p ISBN: 0-921689-26-8 $19.95 (pbk.) / ISBN: 0-921689-27-6 $39.95 (bound)

THE CONQUEST OF BREAD *(Volume 4)*

The Conquest of Bread presents the clearest statement of Kropotkin's anarchist social doctrines. In Kropotkin's own description, the book is "a study of humanity, and of the economic means to satisfy them."

235p ISBN: 0-921689-50-0 $19.95 (pbk.) / ISBN: 0-921689-51-9 $38.95 (bound)

RUSSIAN LITERATURE: Ideals and Realities *(Volume 5)*

Kropotkin believed that the best minds of Russia chose literature to express their conceptions of national life and their ideals. His literary history celebrates the golden age of Russian writing.

385p ISBN: 0-921689-84-5 $19.95 (pbk.) / ISBN: 0-921689-85-3 $38.95 (bound)

IN RUSSIAN AND FRENCH PRISONS *(Volume 6)*

Nearly a century has passed since Kropotkin wrote *In Russian and French Prisons*, yet his criticisms of the penal system are still relevant. Although he makes extensive use of the memoirs of former prisoners and the works of contemporary penologists, it is his own experience in prison that gives this book its power.

387p ISBN: 0-921689-98-5 $19.95 (pbk.) / ISBN: 0-921689-99-3 $38.95 (bound)

WORDS OF A REBEL *(Volume 7)*

First published in 1885 in Paris, this collection of articles constitutes Kropotkin's first book. Originally titled *Paroles d'un Révolté,* it includes his earliest works from the period 1879–1882. In the succeeding years it was translated into Italian, Spanish, Bulgarian, Russian, and Chinese. This is the first English-languge translation.

229p ISBN: 1-895431-04-2 (pbk.) $19.95 / ISBN: 1-895431-050 (bound) $29.95

ETHICS *(Volume 8)*

Ethics is the swan song of this great humanitarian scientist and anarchist, and constitutes, as it were, the crowning work and the résumé of all the scientific, philosophical, and sociological views of Peter Kropotkin at which he arrived in the course of his long and unusually rich life.

349 p ISBN: 1-895431-36-0$19.9 5(pbk.) / ISBN: 1-895431-37-9$38.95 (bound)

PETER KROPOTKIN: From Prince To Rebel
(Special to the Collection)

by George Woodcock and Ivan Avakumovic

In this special addition to the collection, Woodcock and Avakumovic present the most significant aspects of Kropotkin's life and thought.

490pISBN: 0-921689-60-8 $19.95 (pbk.) / ISBN: 0-921689 61 6 $38.95 (bound)

Forthcoming ...

FIELDS, FACTORIES AND WORKSHOPS *(Volume 9)*

Kropotkin's views on the future of world resources and people's working lives.

255p ISBN: 0-921689-38-7 $19.95 (pbk.) / ISBN: 0-921689-39-5 $38.95 (bound)

FUGITIVE WRITINGS *(Volume 10)*

A compilation of pamphlets and essays embracing Kropotkin's philosophy. The material consists of essays that either have not been previously published, or have been out of print since their original publication.

240p ISBN: 0-921689-42-5 $19.95 / ISBN: 0-921689-43-3 $38.95 (bound)

EVOLUTION AND ENVIRONMENT *(Volume 11)*

Seven essays on evolution, written between 1910 and 1915, never before published.

255p ISBN: 0-921689-44-1 $19.95 / ISBN: 0-921689-45-X $38.95 (bound)

BLACK ROSE BOOKS

has published the following books of related interests

Emma Goldman: Sexuality and the Impurity of the State, *by Bonnie Haaland*
The Nature of Co-operation, *by John G. Craig*
Civilization and Its Discontented, *by John E. Laffey*
Dissidence: Essays Against the Mainstream, *by Dimitrios Roussopoulos*
Bakunin on Anarchism, *edited by Sam Dolgoff*
Political Arrangements, *edited by Henri Lustiger-Thaler*
Toward a Humanist Political Economy, *by Harold Chorney and Phillip Hansen*
From the Ground Up: Essays on Grassroots and Workplace Democracy, *by C. George Benello*
Urbanization Without Cities, *by Murray Bookchin*
The Geography of Freedom: The Odyssey of Elisée Reclus, *by Marie Fleming*
Freedom and Authority, *by William R. McKercher*
The Anarchist Moment: Reflections on Culture, Nature and Power, *by John Clark*
Year 501: The Conquest Continues, *by Noam Chomsky*
Rethinking Camelot, JFK, the Vietnam War, and US Political Culture, *by Noam Chomsky*
Language and Politics, *by Noam Chomsky, edited by Carlos P. Otero*
The Political Economy of Human Rights, Vol. 1. The Washington Connection and Third World Fascism, *by Noam Chomksy and Edward S. Herman*
The Politics of Euro-Communism, *edited by Carl Boggs and David Plotke,*
The Modern State: An Anarchist Analysis, *by Frank Harrison*
Post-Scarcity Anarchism, *by Murray Bookchin*
Toward an Ecological Society, *by Murray Bookchin*
The State, *by Franz Oppenheimer*
Anarchist Organization: The History of the FAI, *by Juan Gòmez Casas*

Send for our free catalogue of books
BLACK ROSE BOOKS
C.P. 1258, Succ. Place du Parc
Montréal, Québec
H2W 2R3 Canada

Printed by
the workers of
Les Ateliers Graphiques Marc Veilleux Inc.
Cap-Saint-Ignace, Québec
for
BLACK ROSE BOOKS ⑤